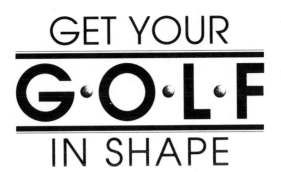

GET YOUR
G·O·L·F
IN SHAPE

GET YOUR
G·O·L·F
IN SHAPE

 Springfield
Books Limited

Published by Springfield Books Limited,
Norman Road, Denby Dale, Huddersfield
HD8 8TH, West Yorkshire, England

©SP Creative Design 1992

Designed and produced by SP Creative Design
Linden House, Kings Road, Bury St Edmunds
Suffolk IP33 3DJ, England

Art director: Rolando Ugolini
Editor: Heather Thomas
Illustrations: Laurence Scarlett and Rolando Ugolini
Photographs: Mark Shearman

First edition 1992

British Library Cataloguing in Publication Data

Get Your Golf in Shape: Complete Guide to
Improving Your Game
    796.352
    ISBN 1-85688-030-3

Typeset in Stone Serif by Halcyon Type & Design Ltd, Ipswich, Suffolk, England
Colour origination by Graphicolour, Thurston, Suffolk, England
Printed and bound by William Clowes Limited, Beccles, Suffolk, England

Contents

The contributors

Alasdair Barr has been the Golf Professional at Gerrards Cross Golf Club, England, since 1974. He is both a Senior Swing Instructor and Senior Swing Examiner for the PGA Training School. In 1987 he became the National Coach to the English Golf Union and he also coaches the Berkshire, Buckinghamshire and Oxfordshire Senior, Junior and Ladies' County teams.

Andrew Brooks is Head Professional at Woodlands Manor Golf Club, Kent, England and is very experienced in teaching club players of all ages and standards.

Craig DeFoy is the Golf Professional at Combe Hill Golf Club, Surrey, England. He was a tournament player on the European circuit for many years and represented Wales seven times in the World Cup. He is now the Welsh National Coach.

David Dunk is the Golf Professional at Cannock Park Golf Club, Staffordshire, England. He has twice represented Great Britain and Ireland in the PGA Cup Matches against the United States and finished as leading Club Professional in the 1984 British Open.

Les Jones is the Golf Professional at Woodbridge Golf Club, Suffolk, England. He is the Head of the Swing Department for the PGA Tutorial Body.

Mick Notley is the Teaching Professional at Windermere Golf Club, Cumbria, England. His professional career began in the 1960s when he played on the European Tour for several years. He then turned to teaching and now runs summer schools at Windermere in conjunction with the Sports Council.

Mark Thomas is the Golf Professional at Parkstone Golf Club, Dorset, England. He played for several years on the European Tour and has twice been West Region PGA Champion.

Alan Thompson is the Golf Professional at Heswall Golf Club, Merseyside, England. After playing for several years on the European Tour, he decided to concentrate on teaching. He is the Cheshire County coach and has coached six England junior internationals.

Chapter One

Equipment

by David Dunk

As in most sports, the golfing equipment you use will have a bearing on how you play and, to a certain extent, how much you enjoy the game of golf. The correct equipment can go a long way to help you achieve your goal of playing satisfying golf to the best of your ability. With this incredible game comes a wide range of equipment intended to help you round the course in the lowest possible score while keeping you warm, dry and comfortable – golf clubs, clothing, shoes, gloves and grips to mention but a few. The choice is bewildering, and you might find it helpful to read the following sections on what to look for initially and how to maintain your equipment.

There are many items that manufacturers claim will help you to lower your score, but I am only going to deal with equipment that *works*. A lot of golfers spend a great deal of money on expensive equipment which will be stored away in the loft or garage after a few weeks. As a young assistant over twenty years ago, I was fussing one day over a set of clubs that an old rep had brought into the shop. "I think they are great," I said. "Don't they look fantastic?"

"Laddie," he said, knowing that I was a fair player, "there are clubs for selling and there are clubs for playing with; these are for selling!"

Golf clubs

These are the most important golf equipment you own. There are so many designs of clubs that it can be somewhat daunting to walk into a well stocked golf shop especially if you are starting out in the game and haven't much idea of what you are looking for, and here the guidance of an experienced professional can be invaluable. Of course, you will want to shop around for the best prices and deals, but do ask your pro

Listed below are some of the factors that need to be taken into account when buying clubs:

Heads – 3 types: peripheral weighted, low profile and blade

Shafts – steel, graphite, boron and titanium

Grips – normal composite, all weather, half cord and full cord

The lie of the club – i.e. the angle at which the shaft comes out of the head

Loft of the club – strong, normal, weak

Flex of shaft – ladies, 'A' or retired gent, medium or 'R' (Regular) regular stiff, stiff, X stiff and double X stiff

Dead weight of club – light, normal and heavy

Swing weight – let's call it 20

Combine all these factors and you can see what a difficult decision it can be when making your choice. So let us examine this in detail and concentrate on the major factors, starting with the complete beginner and then working up to the single-figure handicapper.

Peripheral-weighted club head

Conventional club head

The peripheral-weighted club (top) is hollowed out at the back of the club giving it a larger sweet spot than that of the conventional club (above).

for advice as he can save you a lot of money and frustration in the long run. The odds against you buying the perfect set of clubs are thousands to one, and you may not be in a position to buy a custom-made set as they can be expensive.

Just starting

Golf clubs can be acquired in a number of ways – you can even buy them out of a catalogue. Second-hand clubs are advertised in the newspapers, relatives may have an old set in the garage, or you may visit your local professional's shop for a second-hand set or some new clubs at the less expensive end of the scale. But here lies a warning! Many golfers who have been playing for years continue trying to play with clubs that are unsuitable, and it becomes increasingly difficult to break the bad habits they have fallen into. In other words, the golfer is trying to suit the clubs whereas the clubs should suit the player.

In both irons and woods/metal woods there are two main metals: zinc/alloy in cheaper clubs, and stainless steel in high-quality ones. If you can afford them, always opt for stainless steel, or make do with less clubs and build up your set as you can afford it – you can purchase many models individually. This is not to say that the zinc/alloy clubs are poor value for money, but they do tend to mark easily, and nor do they hold their second-hand value well.

Both irons and woods can be made out of zinc/alloy or stainless steel. Better quality metals can be found in some of the less expensive sets; in irons 430 stainless, and in woods 17.4 PH are the most common and give excellent value for money.

Peripheral - weighted clubs

Without doubt you should be looking for clubs that are peripheral weighted, i.e. the back of the club is hollowed out. This system really does work; look at the illustration of a conventional iron head and a peripheral-weighted head. You will see from the shaded areas of the sweet spot that it is significantly larger on the peripheral-weighted head and it is also expanded wider (see page 9).

When it comes to woods, the peripheral weight is built into the club. The very make-up of a metal wood accounts for the peripheral weight as the head is cast hollow with the centre filled in later with expanded polyurethane foam.

Combine the peripheral weight of a metal wood and the lower centre of gravity, because of a weighted sole plate, and you have a wood not only a little more accurate but one that also lifts the ball higher due to the lower centre of gravity. In general, these give a better performance than the traditional woods.

It may be helpful to consider how the clubs are set up. Most off-the-shelf clubs are made for a person of average height. The two most important considerations are the lie of the club, and the shaft. The lie of the clubs in the irons is particularly important because you have to take a divot. For example, if the club is too flat for you, you are too tall for your clubs and the toe of the club will dig into the ground at impact and try and open the club face as you swing through the shot.

In other words, with a standard 5 iron the lie of the club should be about 60 degrees; but if you are tall 62 degrees would probably suit you, whereas 58 degrees would be better if you are shorter. When you are in

The lie of the club is very important. If the club is too flat for you (far right) the toe will dig into the ground at impact. The 5 irons (right) illustrate the correct lie related to your height: 62° (upright) if you are tall; 60° (normal) if you are of medium height; and 58° (flat) if you are on the short side.

your address position, the toe of the club should be slightly off the ground because when you swing, centrifugal force sends your arms slightly away from your body and the shaft of the club bends on your downswing. These two forces working together will bring the leading edge of the club through square to the ground.

Golf shafts

There are four main types of golf shaft, but although new materials are coming onto the scene all the time, so far none have been able to out-perform the steel shaft. It seems to be the most consistent out of all the shafts now available and is found at the cheaper end of the range. The flex of the shaft is also relevant; basically slow swingers benefit from the use of flexible shafts whereas fast swingers (i.e. big hitters) perform better with stiffer shafts. For the beginner, this may not be too important, but when you start to become more consistent in your game and breaking your magical figure, whether it is 120, 110 or the big 100, is your objective, then more suitable shafts start to come into their own, and you should experiment with different types or seek the advice of your golf professional.

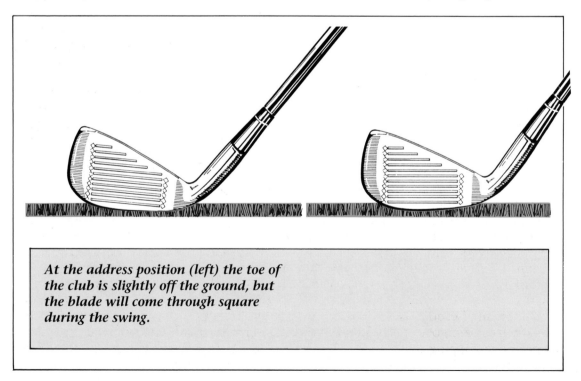

At the address position (left) the toe of the club is slightly off the ground, but the blade will come through square during the swing.

The club head and grips

Peripheral weighted, cavity backed and perimeter weighted are the club heads to look for, preferably in stainless steel with a cavity in the rear of the blade.

Grips are a very important part of the golf club as they are your only physical contact with the club, so it is obvious that old, worn or ill-fitting grips can be a big disadvantage. For instance, if a shot is hit off the toe or heel of the club, the club itself will try and twist in your hand resulting in an exaggerated bad shot. We do not use the centre of the club very often – this is especially true of beginners and high handicappers – so many shots can deviate if your grip contact with the golf club is not good. However, with the right grip, the ball will not go as far off-line.

Weather conditions must also be taken into account; you can buy all-weather grips, but until you have tried a variety of these in different conditions you probably will not know which suit you best.

To a large extent grips are a personal thing; there are the normal rubber grips, those that are made of different compounds, and half cord and full cord grips. These are the main varieties you are likely to encounter, but do be advised by your PGA professional if you are unsure about which one to choose.

If buying second-hand clubs, check that the grips are good, it could save you money on re-gripping at a later date. If they look as though they need replacing, then

tell the owner or retailer that you would consider buying them only if they were re-gripped. You should then get an offer to re-grip them at a reduced price.

Size is another factor: large hands need thick grips, whereas small hands require slim ones. If the grip does not fit your hand, you cannot hold the club correctly and this will result in poor performance. A good way of checking the thickness is to take your normal grip on the club, then take away your right hand and look at the tips of the fingers on your left hand. If they are digging into the palm of your hand near your thumb, then the grip is too thin for you and you will not be able to obtain the correct amount of purchase on the grip. Too thin a grip can also allow your left hand to go over too far and put it into a strong position with the probability of hooking the ball. However, if the grip is too thick, you will find a gap between your fingers and your hand, and usually this prompts you to place the thumb of your left hand straight down the middle of the grip instead of slightly over to the right, thus encouraging a slice or fade. With the perfect grip, the fingers and hand should just touch.

Grip thickness

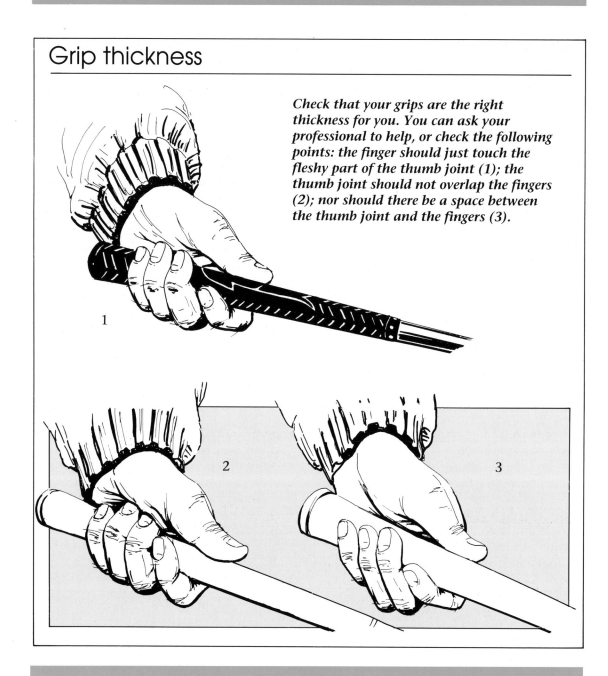

Check that your grips are the right thickness for you. You can ask your professional to help, or check the following points: the finger should just touch the fleshy part of the thumb joint (1); the thumb joint should not overlap the fingers (2); nor should there be a space between the thumb joint and the fingers (3).

1

2

3

Swing weights

The swing weight of the club becomes more important as your game improves. It is the balance or fulcrum of the club at a point about 14 inches from the top of the grip. This enables us to determine the relevant weight of the club during the swing. A heavy club head will take the swing weight up, while a lighter head will bring it down. These swing weights are measured in letters and numbers, the most used letters being 'C' and 'D'. Within each letter there are 10 numbers on a scale of 0 - 9. Thus C6 is lighter than C7, and after C9 there are D0, D1, D2 etc.

Modern clubs have decreased in swing weight over the last decade with the accent being on speed – a lighter club is easier to swing and can create a greater club head speed. Some manufacturers do not identify swing weights on any of their clubs in the lower price range, and hence the fact that although the numbers on the bottom say 3,

4, 5, 6 etc., the distance of the shots from each club will not be of a consistent length. Unfortunately, you cannot see the swing weight of a club so professional advice is essential on this subject.

Putters

The importance of good putting is often overlooked when you start playing golf, but imagine a really good player going round a championship course in a level par 72, which is made up from hitting each green in the allocated number of shots, i.e. 36, and taking two putts on every green making a total of 36 putts. One club – the putter – is used 36 times, whereas the remaining 36 shots are shared between the other thirteen clubs in the bag. So if you are going to be proficient with one club, try and make it the putter.

When choosing one, take a few practice putts before opting for a particular

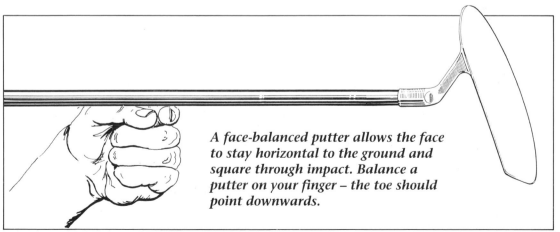

A face-balanced putter allows the face to stay horizontal to the ground and square through impact. Balance a putter on your finger – the toe should point downwards.

model. You must feel comfortable with a putter as soon as you pick it up, and it must look right when you look down, otherwise you probably won't putt well with it.

The quality of the metal and the shaft is not as important in a putter as it is in your irons and woods, although a very whippy shaft is unlikely to perform very well. Try and ensure that the bottom of the putter lies flat on the ground when you are in your normal address position and that the grip is comfortable in your hand.

Face balancing can help you to putt better and more consistently. This allows the face of the putter to go through impact as square as possible. Try balancing a putter over your finger and you will find that the toe of the putter points down to the ground. In other words, the toe of the putter is heavier than the heel. A face-balanced putter will help the face to stay square through impact.

Professional tip

Lines on the top and back of the putter can also be helpful. They enable you to achieve the same eye position every time you address the ball, thereby creating a consistent address position.

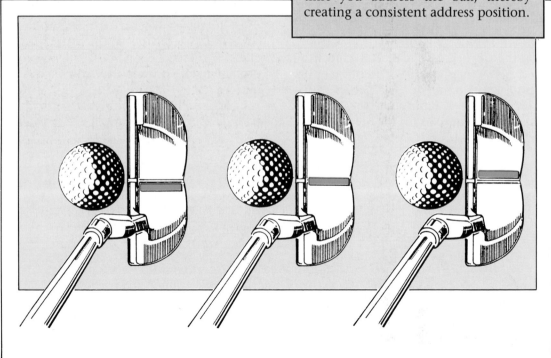

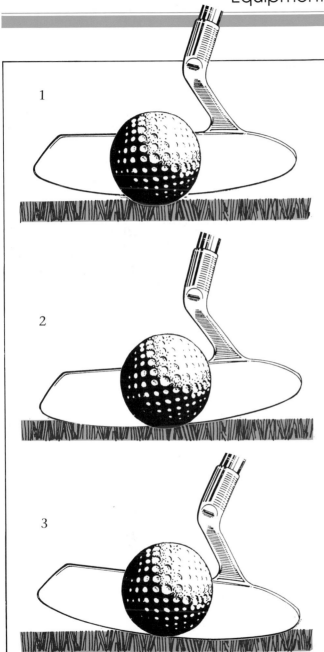

1

2

3

Note how the putter head is horizontal to the ground (1) and square at impact. The bottom should lie flat on the ground at address – not pointing downwards (2) or upwards (3).

Maintaining your clubs

General maintenance of your golf clubs will help to keep them in good condition and could even influence the way you play. Cleaning with soap and water is adequate for looking after both irons and woods. The wooden wood has almost been made redundant now. In the past, you could rub down your old wood with sand paper, stain the head and re-varnish it for the new season. Of course, this is not possible with the metal woods, although they can begin to look the worse for wear after a while. When this happens, they can be re-sandblasted in some pro shops.

If you use iron covers for your irons as well as head covers for your woods, do take care to remove them after playing. In certain circumstances, the covers may hold moisture and can act like a mini-greenhouse. Although your clubs should not rust, they may tarnish, usually where minute deposits of the sand blasting material has been left behind. If this should happen, a light buffing with some wire wool normally puts things right.

A grooving tool is useful for scraping and brushing dirt from the club face.

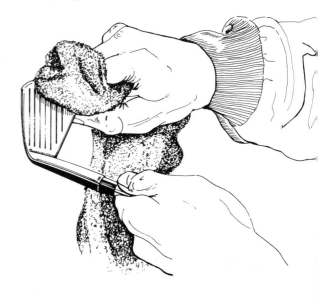

Waterproofs

When choosing your waterproofs it is worth bearing in mind that whereas some suits 'breathe' others do not, and these can get quite uncomfortable when perspiration builds up. Unfortunately, the cost of a suit is related to its quality, and while breathable suits are expensive, they really do work and keep you warm and dry inside. Most manufacturers cut the material in such a way that you can swing freely with the emphasis on shoulder and arm movement. A good tip to remember when buying a suit is to try it on over a sweater. On really cold days you may need one, and even if the suit feels comfortable in the shop it could be a little tight if it does not fit snugly over a sweater. A tight

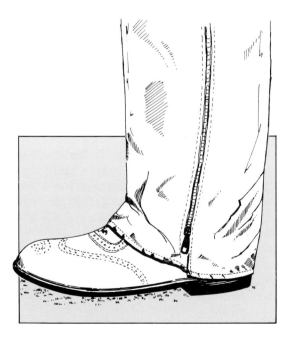

suit will restrict the air flow around the body, which helps to keep you warm. One other feature to look for is the way in which the pockets are cut. Rain should not be able to get into the pockets. The well-designed suit will have pockets covered with a flap allowing the rain to continue down the suit. The length of the trousers is also important as a longer length will allow the water to run onto your shoe rather than into it, as is the case with shorter trousers.

Shoes

Four or five miles is a long way to walk, and a good pair of golf shoes is essential. When starting out in golf, it is understandable that you will not want to spend a fortune, so with this in mind a cheap pair of rubber waterproof shoes is the most popular buy – even the most experienced golfer will probably have a pair of these in his locker for very wet days. However, like some of the cheaper waterproof suits, they do not allow your feet to breathe properly and can get hot and sticky. Further up the scale come leather shoes. Most have a composite sole rather than a leather one which makes them easy to look after. Leather soles do not wear so well and are very heavy in comparison. After a couple of years of damp weather golfing, they can take a fearful battering and tend to curl up, making the shoes quite uncomfortable. The leather upper is not completely waterproof and will let water in eventually, although some have a waterproof lining, which is like an inner sock. This type of shoe costs more than the normal sort, so be sure to check the length of the guarantee as some are guaranteed waterproof for six months only!

Golf gloves

Golf gloves are important only if you feel comfortable wearing them. A few of the top tournament pros do not wear gloves, but, as you will have noticed, many of them do. A good-fitting glove will help keep a good contact with your grip, which, in turn, will result in better shots. When buying a glove, make sure that it fits tightly and that the palm of the glove is taut at all times. Choose a glove with elastic stitched into the back and also on the velcro fastening so that when the glove begins to stretch with wear you can continue to pull the palm tight.

Gloves are made out of two types of materials – leather and synthetic (all-weather) leather. Leather gloves are the most expensive, and although manufacturers will tell you that their all-weather gloves are reliable in every weather condition, I feel that you cannot beat a good leather glove in reasonably dry conditions. However, the all-weather glove is probably better in very wet conditions. One other benefit of the all-weather glove is that you can wash it out when it gets soiled; leather has to be dried very slowly and never feels the same again after a soaking.

Professional tip

If your shoes have steel spikes take them out and put a drop of grease into each socket. The shoes should outlive the spikes and they have a habit of rusting in when they need to be removed, thereby damaging the sole of the shoe. The best studs are the ones with nylon threads; not only are they lighter but also they do not rust into the shoes. Unfortunately, they are not successful when put into a steel socket.

Chapter Two

Warm-up routines and practice

Many golfers look forward all week to their weekend game of golf, and when they arrive at the course they head straight for the first tee and hit that vital shot without any warm-up or preparation. This is possibly the most important shot of the round yet they dash onto the tee and may even hook or slice it. A well-hit drive now down the middle of the fairway gives you confidence and shows your playing partners that you are on good form and playing to, or even below, your handicap.

Warming up and hitting a few practice balls before you play will help you to play better and more confidently out on the course. The top professionals always warm up before a match, and if it helps them, it can help you, too. It is a good idea to start off with a few chips and/or pitches with a wedge, and then work up through the irons and eventually finish by hitting some shots with a driver.

If a practice pitch is available, this is a good way of loosening up and brushing up on your basic technique. It may help you to iron out any faults that have crept into your game or give you an opportunity to try out a new tip or piece of advice from your pro. If a practice pitch is not available, then look for a practice net, which is nearly as good. You will approach the first tee with more confidence if you hit a few shots into the net beforehand.

Practice also helps to ingrain the fundamental skills of golf so that they become automatic to you, and you do not have to think consciously about what you are doing when you swing, putt or chip, for

instance. However, you should practise to some purpose and not just hit balls aimlessly – this will not improve your game. Rather, in your practice, you should attempt to simulate your real play and the situations you encounter out on the course. If there is a bunker, you can practise hitting shots onto the green, or you could try chipping, pitching and putting from various positions around the green, concentrating on aiming for the centre of the green to get down in two, rather than going straight for the hole. Do not look on your practice as a chore, but rather as an interesting and enjoyable session which will reap results out on the course later. Here are some drills for you to try out next time you play golf.

Warm-up exercises

Performing some stretching and loosening exercises before playing a round of golf will stretch out your muscles gently and get them ready for the game to come. They will increase flexibility and help you to develop your full potential in the golf swing with maximum rotation. They also reduce the risk of injury by warming the muscles up ready for action. If you charge out and start swinging while your muscles are cold or tense, there is always the danger that you may pull or strain them. Warming up need take only a few minutes so it is worth arriving a little early for your game so that you can perform some of the following exercises first. Even in the car on the way, you can practise squeezing the steering wheel to help strengthen your hand and wrist muscles!

Club across shoulders exercise

This exercise not only loosens your trunk but also helps to promote weight transference onto the right leg on the backswing turn, and the left leg on the follow through. Place your club shaft across your shoulders and press it against your shoulders with your left forearm crossing over your right arm. Now, with your left hand, push the right shoulder back until the line of the shaft has turned through approximately 90 degrees. At the same time, keep your head steady.

Then turn your shoulders the opposite way and, as you do so, your right knee and foot and hips should move to the left to mimic the action of a normal swing – feel the weight transference. Repeat the exercise to the other side and do 5 repetitions each side.

Club swinging exercise

Use a two-handed grip to hold your 2 and 3 irons (or 3 and 4 irons) together, and swing them slowly and rhythmically. They will feel quite heavy so start off with short swings and build up to longer and eventually full swings. This exercise helps strengthen the golfing muscles in your hands and arms.

Arm loosening exercise

No amount of practice swinging gets you completely ready to hit the ball, but this simple exercise can help loosen your forearms. Find a patch of rough or long grass away from the playing area. Take a 4 or 5 iron and swing away at the long grass. The fact that your club head is coming in contact with a stationary object will prepare your hand and forearm for your important first shot off the tee.

Club across hips exercise

Hold the club shaft across your hips in both hands with your thumbs against each hip joint pointing inwards towards your body. Push your right hip backwards and make a backswing turn. Then push your left hip back and make a follow through. Feel your hips rotating as you do so, and your weight transferring from the right to the left leg as in a normal swing.

Club behind neck exercise

Stand with your feet apart and knees slightly flexed. Hold the shaft of the club behind your neck. Keep your head upright and hold the club shaft with the palms of the hands forwards. Now turn to the right, rotating from the hips and keeping the right leg and foot in the same position. Do not allow the left heel to rise off the ground. Repeat 5 times on each side.

Club behind back exercise

This exercise simulates the action of the swing and stretches out your golfing muscles. Place a club behind your back and lock it in place with your arms over the shaft, seated at your elbows. Assume your normal address position and rotate your shoulders and hips as though you were making a backswing. Feel the stretch in your muscles, then rotate to the other side as if you were on the follow through. Keep rotating slowly and rhythmically from side to side until your trunk and shoulders have loosened up. Use your legs to transfer your weight as in a normal swing.

Hand and arm strengthening exercises

1 With a squash ball

Take a squash ball in each hand and squeeze hard and rhythmically. If you are right-handed, concentrate particularly on strengthening your left hand (or vice versa).

2 With a weight

Tie a light weight onto the end of a piece of string and attach the other end of the string to a piece of wood. Hold the wood in both hands out in front of you at shoulder height with both arms outstretched and palms facing downwards. Slowly wind the weight up and down.

Chapter Three

Fit for Golf
by Alan Thompson

These days, with the aid of buggies, electric trollies, caddy carts and the old fashioned caddy, there are not many people who are incapable of walking a golf course and playing 18 holes of golf. General fitness is not covered here but it is obviously beneficial to be reasonably fit and able to achieve this comfortably. I remember as a young man asking my doctor, a keen and good golfer, to recommend some strengthening exercises for golf. His reply was, "The only exercise for golf is golf". However, I am going to recommend a few exercises that will help you to do the following:

1 Develop better golf technique.

2 Strengthen the golf muscles. The aim is to achieve a wiry, supple strength, not 'Mr Universe' strength.

Body turn

This movement is the axle of the swing, and few people master it. Performing the following exercise regularly will help you to improve your body turn.

Exercise

With your back to a wall, address an imaginary ball. Your heels should be six inches from the wall and your backside will *just* touch it. Mark the wall with a vertical line to correspond with your spine and a horizontal line at eye level at address (1). Now you turn as per the backswing and touch the vertical line with your right elbow, and the horizontal line with the left hand. You will achieve a 90 degree backswing turn (2). Now you turn back through address and reverse to touch the vertical line with your left elbow and the horizontal line with the right hand. You will achieve a 90 degree throughswing turn (3). The elbows should touch the vertical line the length of your forearm below the horizontal line.

Weight transfer

As the body rotates through the backswing and throughswing, the weight should shift or transfer from even at address to 80:20 favouring the right leg at the end of the backswing, through to 100 per cent on the left leg at the end of the throughswing.

Use this exercise to introduce the turn and loosen up the muscles involved. After a while the initial strain will give way to suppleness. As you become more advanced, examine it in more detail – notice how the angle of the spine is constant from address

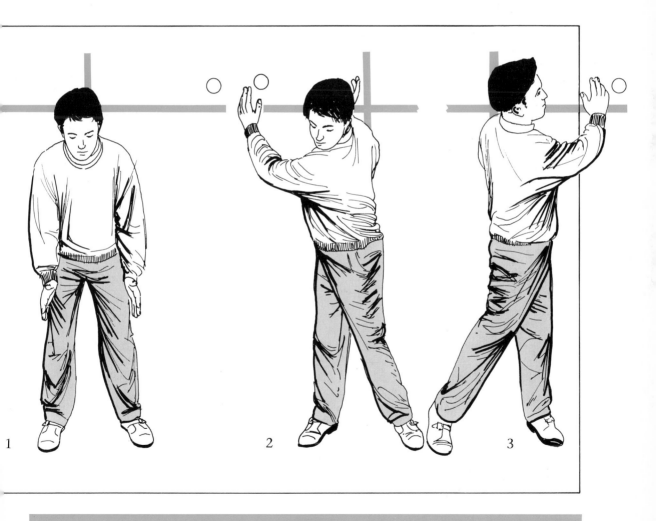

1   2   3

throughout the exercise – an absolute fundamental of the game.

Notice how the elbows fold right in the backswing, left in the followthrough (not maintained straight as is a common misconception). Notice how the hands and arms go over the right shoulder in the backswing and over the left shoulder in the throughswing. Use the address as a reference for impact.

Hands

Exercise

Stand with your feet together and your back to the wall. Swing the club from address to a position where the left arm is horizontal in the backswing. The club should be at approximately 90 degrees to the left arm, and the shoulders should have turned about 45 degrees (1). Now reverse and swing the club through address and on into the throughswing so that the right arm is horizontal and the club shaft is at 90 degrees to the right arm. Again, turn your shoulders approximately 45 degrees into the throughswing (2). The shaft angle is very important in this exercise, and it is a good opportunity to get this right. It should point through the right shoulder to a point just inside the ball (3) and should not touch the wall in the backswing.

Object

Good technique training demonstrates and manipulates both the hingeing of the wrists and the relationship with the shoulder turn. For *physical strength*, this exercise should be performed with a weighted club and repeated several times. It is very good for

strengthening hands and forearms, and helps relieve problems such as failing to hold onto the club in the left hand at the top of the backswing.

Now run both exercises into one, i.e. employ the shoulder turn as in the first exercise, and the hand and arm action from the second exercise. Again, a weighted club converts the exercise from a pure technique practice to one that will also improve your physical strength. The weighted club also helps to promote the 'swinging' aspect of the technique rather than just manoeuvring the club through a series of positions, which is an easy trap to fall into initially. Try to feel the *co-ordination* of a good swing.

Legs

Leg action – right leg

As you work on the first two exercises and begin to use the right type of movements, you can progress to trying to improve the action and role of your legs within the swing. Initially it is important to see that they move correctly in response to the turn of your body. If you visualize that your feet are virtually static during the swing and your shoulders turn through 90 degrees, then you can see that there is a gradual turn of the body from the feet upwards. In the backswing the role of the legs is to discipline this turn. To achieve this the right knee *resists* the turn of the shoulders by remaining still and flexed, as at address.

Physical strength

This is a trick of technique rather than strength, but again repetitious practice with a weighted club is best.

Exercise-technique practice

At address, place a chair against the right knee as shown here. Complete the backswing turn without disturbing the chair by moving or straightening the right knee. The right leg is now functioning correctly in the swing, i.e. carrying 80 per cent of your weight and doing so without billowing out to the right or straightening back under the turn. At first this is likely to prove quite difficult but, as ever, practice will prevail.

Leg action – left leg

Where your legs resisted in the backswing, they do not *resist* in the throughswing. Instead they clear out of the way by shifting (moving towards the target) a little and turning a lot. The common mistakes in this area are often made by youngsters, who tend to shift too much to the left, and in older people who may not shift at all. Correctly, the right leg moves towards the target in the downswing as the body unwinds but only sufficiently for the weight to move to the left leg. The predominant movement is rotational. **Remember:** a little shift and a lot of turn.

Exercise

Turn the chair round and place it against your left heel, with the back near your left hip. Complete the throughswing so that you just touch the chair with your left hip at impact, and rotate your hips through to parallel to the back of the chair at the end of the swing. At impact, the left knee will be slightly flexed. At the end of the follow through it will be straight. Your weight should be fully on your left leg.

Physical strength

This is more of a technique than a strength-building exercise, but repetitious practice with a weighted club builds athleticism into the movements. All of these exercises should be used in the same way.

1 To achieve the *correct type of movement*, and at this stage it is better to go for a rough and ready attempt rather than kill the movements with discipline. For instance, in learning a shoulder turn do not worry about maintaining a perfectly still head – it is counter-productive. Allow some leeway in trying to turn and shift the weight. Look at the illustration to see what I mean.

2 Gradually introduce the idea of discipline and thereby polish and streamline the movements.

3 Using a weighted club use the same exercises to strengthen the muscles involved. This aspect of golfing 'strength' helps on all fronts – as the muscles get stronger the movements get better and more disciplined, and the swing generates more distance and accuracy.

Again, remember that you are not trying to body-build with these exercises, and ideally they should be used as a back up to a series of good basic golf lessons. However, if you do use them on a regular basis, i.e. 20 minutes each day, they will help to keep you broadly 'fit for golf' and ready for your weekend round.

Address an imaginary ball with your back to a wall and make a backswing turn. Then reverse to achieve a 90 degree throughswing turn. See page 30 for a fuller explanation of this exercise.

Mental energy

Closely associated with how you feel physically is your state of mind. To give an example of this, I well remember a friend of mine playing in our Club Championship. He had finished a poor morning round with four birdies and two pars in the last six holes, giving himself a faint glimmer of winning the event overall, with a good afternoon score. Buoyed up by this he went to the afternoon round feeling very confident and 'like a two-year-old'. However, two shots out of bounds from the tee added four shots to his score and '100 years' to his age. He played his third tee shot feeling a physical wreck, with hardly enough energy to swing the club. We do rise and fall *physically* with our mood swings.

I am therefore, going to recommend another exercise – a mental exercise that takes the form of a game plan. The day before you are due to play your next round, sit down at home with a card and divide the course into groups of holes: 4 of 4 plus 1 of 2, i.e. 1-4, 5-8, 9-12, 13-16, 17+18. Next, make a realistic assessment of what you may score on each hole, in each group, and make an overall total for each group. The example (right) assumes you have a 17 handicap, but obviously you must use your own handicap when working out your plan.

Notice that there are no birdies and no disasters, but what you have done is realistically 'if'd and butted' your way to 69 nett, 3 under par. Next morning you go out and, let us say, score 19 for the first group. Not bad,

Holes	Par	Est
1	4	5
2	4	5
3	4	4
4	3	4
TOTAL	15	18
5	5	6
6	4	5
7	4	5
8	3	4
TOTAL	16	20
Holes	Par	Est
9	5	6
10	4	5
11	3	3
12	5	6
TOTAL	17	20
13	4	4
14	4	5
15	4	5
16	3	3
TOTAL	15	17
17	5	6
18	4	5
TOTAL	9	11

PAR 72 EST 86-17 = 69

but your overall total is now scheduled for 70. In the next group you take 8 at the fifth, two more than you allowed and, by normal standards, bad enough news to cause further disasters in its wake. However, if you fit it into your schedule you are now only heading for 72, and if you can score perhaps a 4 at either 6 or 7 you score 21 for the group and you are back on a schedule that finishes under par.

The value of this is that the game plan idea allows you to see a 'disaster' in a different light and does not let it destroy your confidence and your mental strength. At the end of that group, the 8 at the fifth has been accommodated and can now be forgotten. It is not a millstone to drag you down for the rest of the round.

From a physical point of view, you are still looking at the round with a view to winning so 'loser's fatigue' does not take hold, and you are still fit and ready to go. Pursue the schedule as best as you can over the next two groups and possibly pick up a shot in one of them. Now your schedule is back to 70 with two holes to play and the schedule allows two bogeys to finish – most golfers would have a chance! Even another 8 stays in the buffer zone. The importance of the right mental approach cannot be over-stated and goes hand-in-hand with the physical side of the game. Follow the physical exercises in this chapter and practise using the game plan, and you will hopefully get fitter both mentally and physically and play better golf.

Chapter Four

Brush up on your technique

by Andrew Brooks

Every time you tee the ball up at the start of another game of golf, you set yourself up for the ups and downs to be expected in a round. How many swing tips will be running through your mind during the next four and a half hours? No doubt someone has told you a very useful tip on which you can draw, but is this really the answer to your problems?

The question that should be in your mind is whether you can improve and build your technique on a number of tips. The answer is simply, 'No'. What you should be doing is brushing up on the basic fundamentals so as to be able to build and improve your overall swing technique.

You should really have only one or two thoughts when you are about to execute a shot, and these should be consistent. To get these key thoughts, you may need to seek the advice of your golf professional, who is fully qualified in such matters. If you are new to golf or just seeking to improve your basic skills and technique, it is important that you see your own professional to build up a relationship with him, and a full understanding of your own swing. The key point for you is that your professional knows and understands your golf swing.

Good golf is all about achieving and retaining consistency, and how can you expect to do this if you have a different thought or feeling every time you hit a shot? When you feel that you have reached a point in your swing when you are not making any progress, or you have a problem such as slicing or hooking, do not jump into the 'Sea of Tips', but search out your PGA professional and get some good, solid advice on which you can work.

So many golfers do not understand swing faults, and by having lessons you will start to develop an understanding of them. Once you understand your faults, you are halfway to rectifying them. How many times do you stand up to a shot and either hook it or slice it, and are you really able to pinpoint what has gone wrong? How many times do you hear people say "Great shot," and the reply: "Thanks – but what did I do differently?" Is that person you? By understanding your swing, you will be able to pinpoint different shots and develop an understanding of what has happened.

The greater your understanding of your swing, the more you will enjoy this great game of golf. Read on and you will find advice on building the basic fundamentals into your set up so that you can check and improve some techniques at address. This is often the most overlooked part of the swing, especially when you are first learning to play. It is no use looking at what is happening in your swing if you do not build a secure, solid base to it. You may have read and seen this illustrated many times, but how many golfers build the set up into their swing? Not many!

> Most people develop faults in their swing from having a faulty set up and this usually leads to trying out many tips and variations, when really they should go back and check the five basic fundamentals.

The 'Sea of Tips'

TRANSFER WEIGHT

MOVE LEFT KNEE

HEAD STEADY

TURN HIPS

Most golfers are given so many tips and well-meaning advice that they can have a destructive effect on their technique – the very opposite of what is intended. If in doubt, consult your Professional and check the basic fundamentals of your set up and swing.

The set up and pre-shot routine

Whether you are a complete novice or an experienced player, you will benefit from the following set-up routine and drills. Practise them regularly to achieve greater consistency in your game.

   The first question to ask yourself is: "When building a house what is the first stage of the production?" Your answer: "The foundations." So we start the golf swing by building the foundations, of which there are five basic fundamental areas. Within those areas there are points to draw upon, and drills for you to practise. Everybody has watched the great tournament pros and seen how effortlessly they execute their shots, yet they all appear to swing differently. One thing you will notice is that the set-up routine for all these great players is similar, and that is why if you do not understand your address position or any part of it, then you must learn it. You will be surprised at how beneficial the results will be. By learning about the five basic fundamentals within the address, and practising some drills to give you a pre-shot routine that you can use and understand, you will achieve greater consistency by repetition of the correct position.

The five basic fundamentals.

Fundamentals

The five basic fundamentals that should be clear in your mind are as follows:
1 Blade position
2 Grip
3 Posture
4 Ball position
5 Alignment

   First of all, read the following, and then, with a club in your hands, follow the instructions.

1 Blade position

This is a very important part of the set up which is often overlooked. To increase the number of straighter shots, you must ensure that the blade is at right angles to the target line. When placing the club behind the ball, picture a line through the line of the ball and see your club at right angles to the target line. You must take care to check that your alignment is correct. You must also make certain that you set the club face with the optimum loft. When placing the blade behind the ball, it is a good idea to support the club with the thumb and forefinger of the right hand. Place the feet together, with the ball and club opposite the big toe on the left foot; the top of the club should be approximately six inches from the top of the inner left thigh, and pointing towards it to give the required distance from the ball.

90°

The club face is square to target line.

The top of the club should be six inches from the top of the inner left thigh pointing towards it.

2 The grip

It is now time to look at placing the hands on the club. At some time or another, you will probably have been given differing advice on this, but the main thing is to keep it simple.

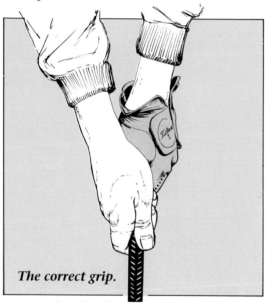

The correct grip.

First of all, what does the grip achieve? It gives us control over the club head as it passes through impact. It also gives us the opportunity to maximize on club head speed. Remember that the intention of the golf swing is to obtain maximum club head speed at impact, in a square to the target line position. Think about that in the 1.8 seconds it takes to complete your swing – it is impossible. So if you set your hands correctly when they are static, they will

provide you with the necessary position at impact. If you want to release the club head squarely along the ball to target line, you must ensure that your hands are in the correct position.

The grip most commonly used is the Vardon grip. When you place the club in your left hand, it should run from the base of the forefinger to the butt of the left hand,

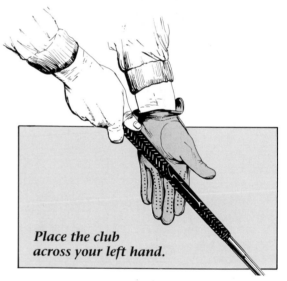

Place the club across your left hand.

¼ inch from the top of the shaft. You then wrap the last three fingers around the grip and squeeze the butt of the club into the butt of the left hand. These three fingers provide the pressure points of the grip. Make sure that the club sits under the fleshy part of the hand. Now wrap the forefinger around the shaft and press the pad of the

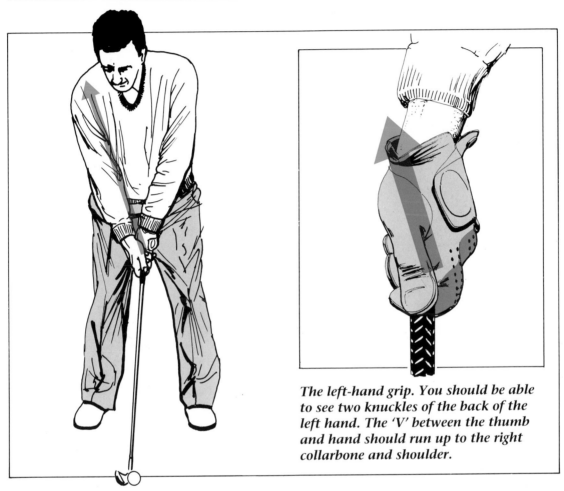

The left-hand grip. You should be able to see two knuckles of the back of the left hand. The 'V' between the thumb and hand should run up to the right collarbone and shoulder.

left thumb onto the right side of the shaft, checking that you can see clearly two knuckles of the back of the left hand. Also make sure that the 'V' between the thumb and hand runs to the collarbone on the right shoulder.

If you have small hands, and this is often the case with women, you may prefer an interlocking grip, although I feel that with larger hands it restricts your power and causes you to grip too firmly. If you feel the need to interlock, you simply point the left forefinger towards the left toe making allowances for the right little finger to interlock. Remember that the left hand is the leading hand, so be sure to practise the left-hand hold, a sure way to increase left-side awareness.

Now bring the right hand into play. If you are using the Vardon grip this is the key point. Place the tip of the little finger, not the knuckle, between the forefinger knuckle and the middle finger of the left hand so that the finger rides on top of the others. This is very important as the majority of people have a tendency to upset the whole balance of the grip by taking the little finger too far into the fingers of the left hand. If you are using the interlocking grip, simply feed the little finger of the right hand between the first and second fingers of the left hand, and hold together softly.

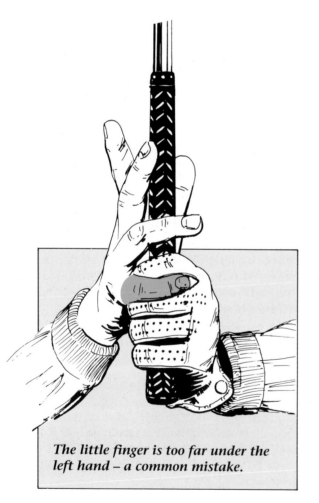

The little finger is too far under the left hand – a common mistake.

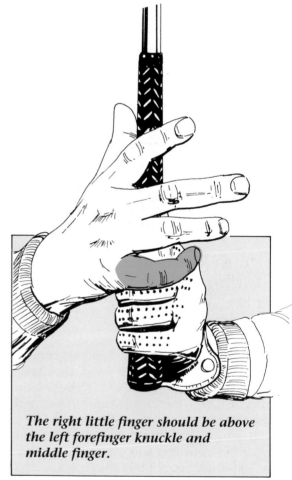

The right little finger should be above the left forefinger knuckle and middle finger.

The interlocking grip: the left forefinger interlocks with the right little finger.

Pressure tip

Take a tube of toothpaste, without its lid, and grip it as you would your club. You should be able to swing it without squeezing toothpaste all over the bathroom!

you should learn it thoroughly and check it constantly. So many beginners fall at this hurdle. Now simply cover the left thumb with the pad of the right hand, resting the thumb comfortably towards the left side of the grip. Then place the forefinger around the shaft, acting as though you were squeezing a trigger, and press very lightly to hold the club in place. Check that the 'V' made between the thumb and hand runs to the collarbone of the right shoulder, and your right hand will now be in neutral position. You will feel as though you are going to let go of the club, but when you first start, this feeling is absolutely necessary. At this stage, check that the back of the left hand and the palm of the right hand face the target area. A large number of golfers fail with right-hand grip problems, and these cause so many faults in the swing.

Remember

Check your two knuckles and your two 'V's, and that the club is positioned in the right place in the hands.

Try to gain a feeling of softness here; many golfers tend to grip too tightly. Now wrap the two middle fingers of the right hand around the shaft making sure that the club rests in the fingers across the middle joints of the fingers and not in the palm of the hand. This position is so important, and

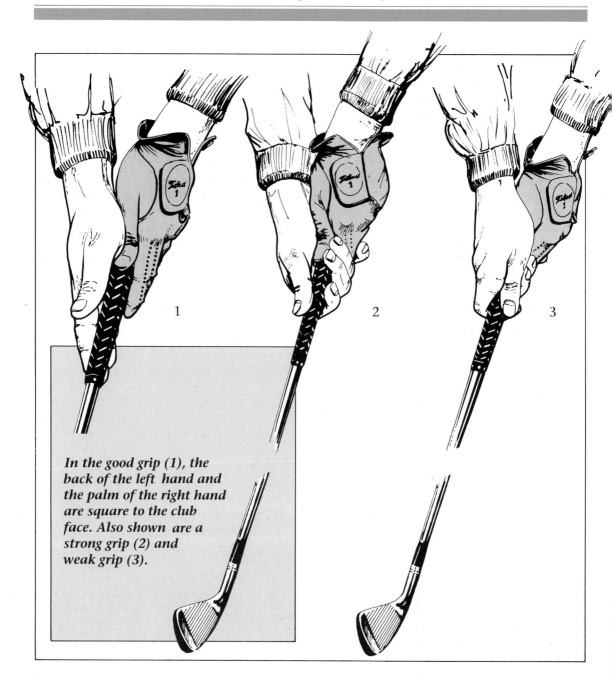

1

2

3

In the good grip (1), the back of the left hand and the palm of the right hand are square to the club face. Also shown are a strong grip (2) and weak grip (3).

3 Posture

When you have mastered the blade position and the grip, you must build the main constituent of your base, which is body posture. This part of the set up is of the utmost importance.

Firstly, you must understand the importance of good posture, which is often overlooked. It is no wonder that some

Good posture is essential for stability and balance during the swing.

golfers hook or slice, as it is good posture that gives you the angle to swing the club along the path to execute the shot. It provides you with the room to swing the hands and arms, thus enabling you to return back to the ball in the position in which you started with the club travelling along the target line. It also provides you with stability and balance, which are essential and influence the basic tempo of the swing. You must take great care in building your posture, and I have developed a technique that I ask all of my pupils to follow and which leads to a greater awareness of the feel of good posture.

Practise the following drill, either in the office or at home, whenever you have a few minutes to spare – in front of a mirror if possible. Stand to attention, with feet together and hands by your sides, palms facing inwards. Now tilt from the hips, feeling your bottom going outwards. Do not hold your bottom in, but be sure to stay relaxed and keep your spine straight. Do not just tilt your chin forwards but actually move your body, holding your chin out from your shoulders throughout. Stop when your shoulders are over the balls of your feet or when you feel the muscles in the back of your knee pulling. As you make this tilt, let the arms fall from the side of your thighs and place your palms together. As you do this, check to see that your hands are hanging beneath your chin. Now let your right hand move three inches lower than your left hand, and let your right shoulder drop lower. Do not force any of your muscles at any time because it will be very difficult to maintain a stretched muscle in a constant position throughout the swing.

All you have to build now is stability to increase the balance in your swing and give you a firm footing on the ground. For my exercise, put your left foot two to three inches to the left, then drop the right foot

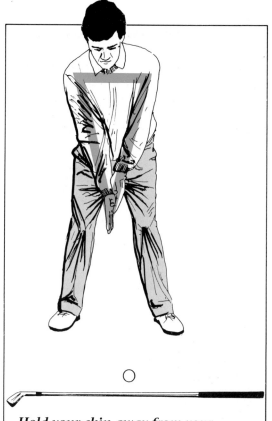

Hold your chin away from your shoulders and point the right elbow towards the right hip.

Good posture: the shoulders, knees and balls of the feet are all in line.

back to approximately shoulder width, keeping your feet parallel. As you do this, make sure that you pass the weight over the balls of the feet and distribute it evenly. I also like to see the knees just comfortably pressing towards each other. This gives greater traction on the ground and also helps to retain a better position during the turn on the backswing.

Comfortably press the elbows together forming a 'V' shape between the arms. A good tip here is to have the left elbow pointing towards the left hip, and the right elbow towards the right hip. Now make sure that you are holding your chin away from the shoulders. This will help to get the hunched look out of your posture. Try and get the feeling of being tall in the chest. Imagine that if you were to drop a plumb line from your shoulder it would pass through the knees and the balls of the feet.

Practise this drill as much as you can and then, when you feel really positive about it, introduce a club, but remember that you cannot build your posture around a golf club – you must build the club into your posture. Look in a mirror to check the position; visual posture is easier to reproduce than feel. If you are not absolutely sure that your clubs are lying correctly, consult your pro. Now that we have established the blade position, the grip to retain the blade and the correct posture to give you stability and room to swing, we will look at ball position.

Now you have set up correctly with good posture, add the club to your set up.

4 Ball position

There are numerous ways to learn ball position and it is obviously of the utmost importance. It allows us to get the ball at the base of the arc and in a position where the club head returns squarely to the target. The wrong ball position can result in all sorts of errors in the shot. If the ball is too far back in the stance, it will fly to the right, or if it is too far forward it can result in a pulled shot. So be sure to use the correct ball position. There are two methods of ball position but, personally, I believe that for beginners and high-handicappers the method of one position for the irons and one for the woods leads to the most consistency.

Irons should be played with the ball opposite a point two to three inches from the inside of the left heel. By altering the right foot for different irons, i.e. with a 7 iron, heel at shoulder width, then every two clubs you go down you increase the stance by about half an inch. So a 3 iron will require a wider stance than a pitching wedge, for example. For consistently straight shots, all irons will be played from approximately two to three inches inside the left heel, and the right foot starts off inside shoulder width for the wedge and increases for every two clubs down you go to approximately two inches outside width for your driver.

The only change you make in your fundamental ball position for woods should be to place the ball opposite the left heel, to encourage you to hit the ball more on the upward swing. All of this is very simple but must be practised and thought about.

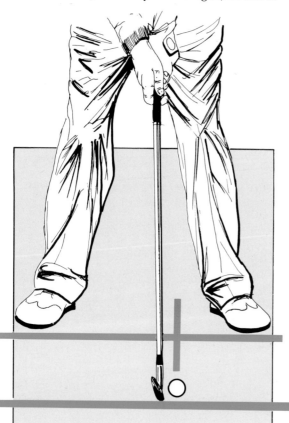

Correct ball position: the ball should be 2-3 inches inside the left heel.

5 Alignment

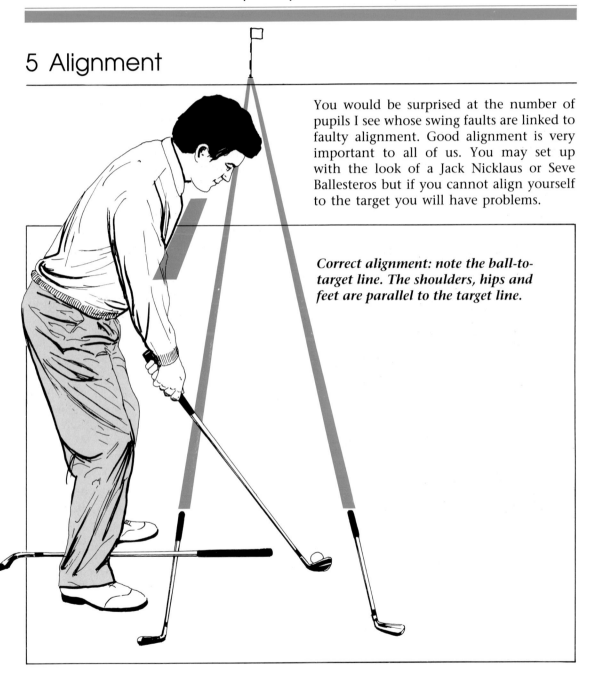

You would be surprised at the number of pupils I see whose swing faults are linked to faulty alignment. Good alignment is very important to all of us. You may set up with the look of a Jack Nicklaus or Seve Ballesteros but if you cannot align yourself to the target you will have problems.

Correct alignment: note the ball-to-target line. The shoulders, hips and feet are parallel to the target line.

The importance of correct alignment procedure is to enable you to release the club head along the given swing path, thus enabling you to maximize on club head speed and direction provided that your other fundamentals are all followed. Now you can see the importance of a square club face, correct grip and posture and ball position, and in that split second at impact all parts are aligned and moving along the correct swing path, thereby enabling a good free-flowing swing action with nothing in the way.

Now I know that probably you have all seen the diagrams of tram lines running to the target and you know the importance of making sure that your club head aims to the target, and your feet, knees, hips and shoulders are all parallel to the target line.

Practice

The drill I use here is very simple. Place your club representing the ball to target line and place another club parallel and, set up on these lines, hit about 15 to 20 shots per session. Engrave in your mind the feeling of being aligned to the target and making certain that you are parallel to the target line. Make sure that all the parts of the body are parallel.

So many amateurs practise without a target in mind. How do you know if you are hitting good shots? Set a target line down, whether you are at the driving range or at your club; it will help you to learn to square up at address. One point to remember any time you fall foul of making the correct body alignment, is that you will alter the shape of your swing. So check your alignment and get your professional to check it too.

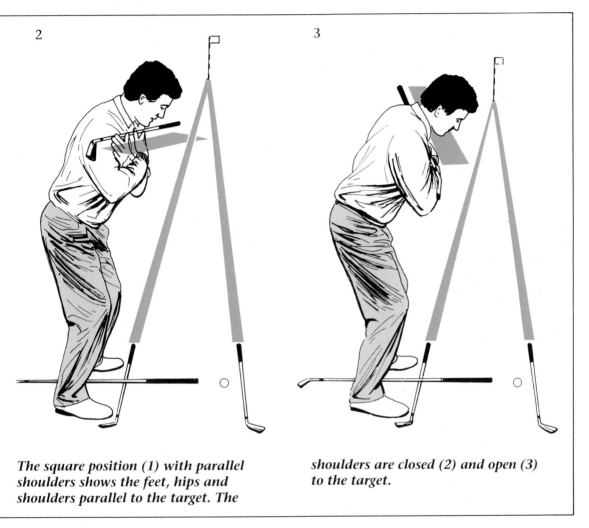

2

3

The square position (1) with parallel shoulders shows the feet, hips and shoulders parallel to the target. The shoulders are closed (2) and open (3) to the target.

Do not aim your shoulders to the target but aim the club face to the target instead, and then set the body up around this position. The biggest fault I encounter in golfers is that they aim to the right; this is simply because in most sports, you tend to have the body behind the projectile. In golf, it is two to three feet away. So as you turn your head to the target, do not line your left shoulder at the target. Line the club and then get your body parallel to the ball-to-target line. Again, practise the drill.

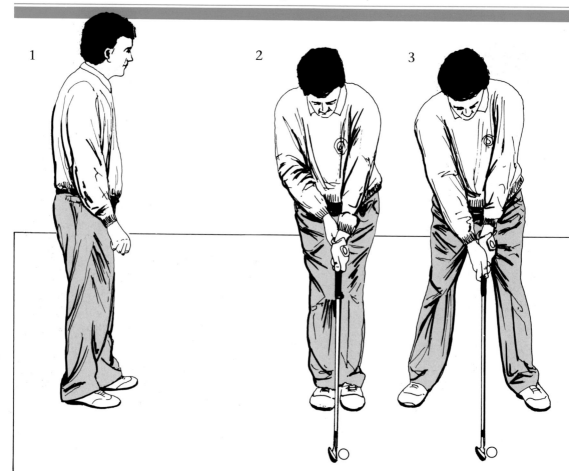

Summary

You now have your five basic funda-mentals and you should practise each one until you are sure of it and you can feel and understand it, and it is ingrained into your pre-shot routine. Now your next practice point is to put these points into sequence and give yourself a good, sound, positive set-up routine. I want you to follow the five illustrations shown here and build up your own routine. It is of the utmost importance to you so as to achieve greater consistency.

Practise this sequence, make it

4

5

The pre-shot routine: take a line from the ball to the target and visualize it by forming a mental picture (1). Square up to the ball (2) with feet together, a set distance away from the ball and place your hands on the grip. Spread your feet (3) and feel the body sink into its practised posture. Look towards the target (4) to check your alignment. Take care to look along the ball-to-target line. Pull the trigger (5) and make your swing.

part of your golf shot, break it down and practise individual parts; but learn it and visualize it, thereby transforming your set up. Hopefully, by referring to some of the basic points above, you will understand and improve your set-up fundamentals. Remember that a good foundation gives the basis of a good, smooth, powerful and balanced swing.

You can transform a poor set up (1) to a good set up (2) with the correct *posture and alignment. It will make all the difference to your shots.*

Chapter Five

Improve your swing technique

by Les Jones

You have been thinking about your golf like so many other golfers before you. You want to play more consistently, reduce your handicap and 'get your golf into shape', but how do you achieve this? We often hear of players who have hit 500 balls on the practice ground and have shown no sign of improvement – why? The answer is that just hitting balls tells you nothing about your golfing skills; you must have disciplines to work on, which will suit you and your game. Your height, build and flexibility will determine your set up and the pattern of your swing – for example, a man of 6ft 4in will appear to swing the club differently to someone of 5ft 6in although they both follow the same technique. So go to the practice ground and be yourself; don't make practice a chore, as it can be enjoyable and exciting. If you develop a good technique, it will lead not only to good performance but also to better scores.

The set up

At set up I like to keep a sequence of blade (aim), hold, ball position, stance and alignment and posture, and when you understand and are happy about these five fundamentals it will be easy to follow and refer to them when you are practising. Always start your practice session with some short shots, and then gradually build up the swing for longer shots.

The pictures show the top of the backswing for golfers of different ages. Your swing is influenced by your suppleness as well as your technique, *strength, height and build. Senior players may not get the shaft parallel (right) but they still generate sufficient power for the downswing.*

The set up for short shots

Using a wedge or 9 iron, set yourself up with the bottom leading edge of the club at right angles to the target and hold it halfway down the grip – this helps control and finesse. The ball should be in the centre of your stance and your stance should be open, which means that the feet and hips point more to the left, while the shoulders remain square. You are now ready to swing the club, and the waggle and forward press are introduced to give you the feeling of being ready for action. The waggle is a backward and forward movement of the club head created by flexing the wrists together with a co-ordinated movement of the feet and legs. The forward press follows these movements with the club head remaining stationary behind the ball while the hips, hands and right knee move slightly towards the target.

The take back

The take back is started with the club head, hands, left arm and left shoulder taking the club back to a waist-high position. The movement of the left shoulder creates sympathetic movements down the left side of the body: the left hip turning, the left knee moving inwards and the left heel rising slightly off the ground. The right hip will move slightly backwards and the right knee will remain flexed as in the set-up position. This co-ordinated movement has transferred the weight from the left to the right side of the body.

Checkpoint

The grip will appear the same as at set up, i.e. two knuckles showing on the left hand at address and two knuckles showing at waist-high. The bottom leading edge of the club will be at right angles to your shoulders.

The downswing

The downswing is initiated by a lateral movement of the hips towards the target and a downward swing of the arms, which releases the club into and through the ball to a waist-high position. During this releasing movement the hips have gone from a lateral into a rotational movement. This creates a natural weight transference back to the left side.

Checkpoint

At waist height both arms and wrists will be straight. The toe of the club will be pointing to the sky and the bottom leading edge will again be at right angles to the shoulders.

These movements must be practised as one, co-ordinated together in a fluid rhythmical movement in order to try and capture the feeling of complete control of the club. Natural progression to the longer clubs stems from this important part of the swing.

Pitch shot (9 iron or wedge)

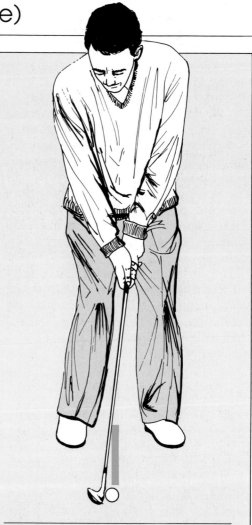

Set up

Here is a good example of preparing yourself for a short pitch shot. All of the afore-mentioned positions show up quite clearly here: the ball position is in the centre of the stance, the hold is a good demonstration of a first-class grip, the left arm is held comfortably straight and the right arm slightly bent. If you study the illustration carefully you will note how relaxed the player appears, giving the feeling of control and confidence. There is no appearance of tension in this set up.

Note: The hold position in relation to the legs. The hands are covering the inside of the left thigh and this position of the hands is used with all the clubs at set up.

Take back

Again with complete relaxation, the club head, hands, arms and shoulders have moved together. There is a slight movement of the left hip and the left knee at this stage but the head has remained central. The face of the club is square, i.e. the toe of the club pointing to the sky.

Note: Again you can see quite clearly the two knuckles the player will see at waist high.

Impact

Here you can see how the lateral hip movement has created the weight transference to the left side and the club has been released to the impact area. Because there is no tension, the head has remained central and the right knee has moved in towards the left. The body has remained behind the ball.

Finished position

The momentum in releasing the club through the ball has carried the player through to the waist-high position. Note that the hips have begun to rotate. The head is just beginning to move slightly avoiding the problem of head down, which causes restriction problems.

Note: The bottom leading edge is at right angles to the shoulders. The grip will be seen to be in the same position as at address.

Pitch shot (different angle)

This sequence of the pitch shot is emphasising the open set up.

Set up

Note here that the set up is the same as above but from this angle you can see clearly that the stance and hips are open. The stance is left of the ball-to-target line, as are the hips but the shoulders are parallel to the ball-to-target line. This is known as the *open* set up used for all short shots.

Take back

The open stance is emphasised from this angle. The square position of the blade and the arms are still comfortably close together. The spinal angle at set up has remained constant at this waist-high position.

Impact and through position

The club head has now been released back squarely and through the ball. The head has begun to move through and the spinal angle is maintained.

The medium irons

The shaft of a medium iron is longer, and therefore you stand further away from the ball and the stance becomes wider to accommodate the longer swing.

The ball position is centre of stance to move into the longer swing, the left shoulder continues to turn and the wrists begin a gradual cocking movement to a three-quarter swing position. The weight has now moved to the right side, the left arm is comfortably straight, the forearms remaining together, the head is central and the spinal angle has remained constant, while the right knee stays flexed. Power is now being felt as the left shoulder turns against the right hip and makes a winding-up movement. Do not mistake this winding-up movement as a physical strength feeling.

The downswing

The downswing follows with the initiating movement of the left hip moving in a lateral direction towards the target. As in all shots this creates a natural weight transference to the left side, the arms moving downwards. Then the club head is released into and through the ball. When the hips become rotational the head begins to come through, and the momentum will carry you through to a finish. When the body is facing the target the arms are together and high in their finish, the right knee has moved towards the left, the right heel is pointing to the sky and you are in balance and control.

Three-quarter shot (with medium iron)

Set up

The address position is the same as that of the short shot but now the stance has become wider to maintain balance and a more powerful winding-up movement. The club being longer, you should be standing further away, and that gives you more radius of swing.

Three-quarter swing

Being a longer club, you are taking it back further into a three-quarter position created by the turning of the left shoulder, and a gradual cocking of the wrists. Note that the right knee has remained flexed, whereas the bigger shoulder turn has given more hip movement, left knee movement and left foot movement. I stress that the last three movements are sympathetic – they happen, you do not make them work.

Impact and follow through

Impact area – again the hips have moved from lateral to rotational. The free release of the club head has left you with the head and right side moving into the ball from behind. The momentum of this movement has carried you through the ball and onwards to a finished position.

Three-quarter shot (different angle)

Address

Here you can see the importance of the posture at set up with the arms hanging comfortably, the back straight but bent from the hips and the knees in a soft relaxed position. This posture now sets the swing plane, i.e. the arc that the club head takes around the body.

Take back

The take back of the club, arms and shoulder has taken you into a position at the top of the swing where the left arm is comfortably straight, right elbow pointing down and the back of the left hand and the club face are related as at address. The arc of the swing is related to the ball-to-target line.

Full swing

With the driver, the ball position will be opposite the left heel and the hold will be ½ inch down the grip. The club being longer means that you will be standing further away from the ball. The stance will also become wider – approximately shoulder width – to maintain balance.

The same factors of the take back apply to the longer swing. As in the short swing the club head will travel lower and wider due to the longer shaft. At waist height, the shoulders continue their turn to 90 degrees, and the wrist action now comes into play with a gradual cocking movement so that the top of the backswing will have been achieved. The hips will have turned 45 degrees and the right knee will remain flexed. These three factors will give you the winding-up feeling; power has then been built into your swing.

Other points to note are that your head remains central, your left arm comfortably straight, the right elbow pointing to the ground to a point behind the right heel, while the spinal angle achieved at address will remain constant.

Impact and follow through

From this good position at the top, the club head has been released into the ball to achieve the now familiar pattern at impact, and the momentum carries you through to the balanced position you are seeking.

Swing plane

The swing plane is set at address by good posture and is the arc made by the club head round the body in the backswing. At the top of the swing your wrists and club face will relate to the correct plane.

Downswing

As in the short game the downswing movements are the same. The momentum created by the longer swing will carry you into and through the ball to a full follow through. The body at this position will be facing the target or slightly left, the weight will be on your left side. With the right knee moving to the left, the right foot will turn so that the back heel of the shoe is pointing to the sky, with hands high and forearms together creating the overall feeling of being well balanced.

Address

As the driver is a longer club, you should be standing further away from the ball, and the ball position in relation to the stance is just inside the left heel. The stance is approximately shoulder width. This set up is the build-up to an ultimate power movement.

Top of backswing

A full 90 degrees shoulder turn has now been achieved with a 45 degrees turn of the hips, and the right knee still remains flexed. Senior and more mature players should note that although the shaft has not reached

Full swing (driver)

parallel, the rest of the movements have still wound up to be in the ultimate power position for someone whose muscles are less supple.

Impact and follow through

Again the release movement has brought you back to the desired impact postion, and the extra momentum acquired by the full turn has given you additional power which has taken you completely through, so that the whole of the body faces the target. Note how the right knee has moved into the left, the weight is solidly on the left side, the right heel is pointing to the sky and there is complete balance. A well-balanced position is a tremendous help in capturing and maintaining rhythm and tempo in your swing. This hold position can be practised so that the swing becomes repetitive.

Driver (at different angle)

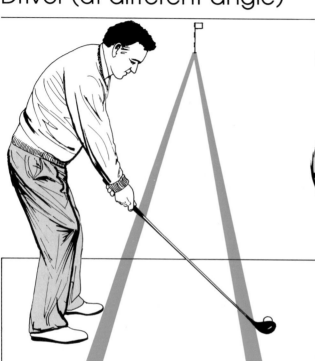

Address

Note the distance of the hands from the body giving complete freedom and room to work the club around the body.

Backswing

The completion of the backswing with wind-up and power movements. Here we can see that the club shaft is parallel to the ball-to-target line and the back of the left hand is related to the club face which, in turn, is related to the swing plane. Note that the spine angle is constant.

Impact

A good demonstration of the moment just before impact. The spinal angle has remained steady as has the head. Lateral and rotational movement of the hips has allowed the arms and wrists to return the blade square, while the right knee has moved in. Note the right shoulder position: it is about to move under the chin giving the right angle of attack with the body weight behind the ball

Follow through

Releasing the club head through impact position to the full follow through. Note the spinal angle has been released to enable freedom of movement to gain this balanced position.

The mental approach

To succeed in the practical skills you have learnt, you will need a mental picture of how to use these skills to reach your goal. Let us examine how you would plan a 30-yard pitch shot over a bunker on to the green. First, your club selection: you may well choose the pitching wedge. Use the bunker positively as a guide to judging the length you wish to pitch the ball, rather than viewing it as a trap that you must try to get over. The loft on your wedge will elevate the ball, so do not try to hit it in such a way as to help it into the air – this is fatal. The length of the shot is governed by the length of the backswing. Decide what you are going to do, visualize the shot you are going to play and then perform it with smoothness and rhythm. Have sufficient courage to practise as many of these shots as your time will allow.

Remember – be sufficiently courageous to keep repeating the shot, and this will give you results, which will bring confidence. A more confident approach will help make you feel more relaxed, and this relaxation promotes the ability to capture the feeling of smoothness and rhythm. This is what golf is all about.

Mid-irons, long irons and woods must be dealt with in the same way. Remember that the moment you set yourself up correctly you are hitting the ball straight. Only your doubts and tensions will prove otherwise; let the swing work, do not attempt to force it to work. Always feel that if you wanted to, you could hit the ball 20 yards further.

Summary

These guidelines are the basic positions and movements to the building up of a classic swing incorporating consistent patterns and built-in power. A tremendous amount of understanding of the skills required can be learnt through reading, and by visiting your PGA professional who can be of tremendous help. He is the person on the spot who will confirm your interpretation of your reading and teach you to make the best of your natural flair and ability. Remember that even champions require constant checking and some even have their 'guru' travelling with them. If they need to practise and check their swings regularly, then you can benefit from doing this too.

Chapter Six

Sharpen up your short game

by Mick Notley

Throughout many years of playing with golfers of all standards, I have learned many lessons. One in particular stands out amongst all others: of all the various departments of the game – driving, fairway woods, long irons etc. – the area in which you can most improve your score is the short game, i.e. chipping and putting.

If you could drive like Seve Ballesteros, you would impress your friends and be the talk of the clubhouse bar, but your handicap would not reduce by as much as you might think. If, however, you were blessed with Seve's short game, your scoring would improve dramatically. The 120 shooter would immediately break 100, and the 10 handicapper would reduce to four.

To be realistic, the driving ability of a Ballesteros, Faldo or Norman is based on a technical skill and athletic prowess which is beyond the reach of 99 per cent or more of the world's golfers. However, in the short game, strength and athleticism are of no particular advantage, and feel and finesse, you may be surprised to learn, are low on your list of priorities.

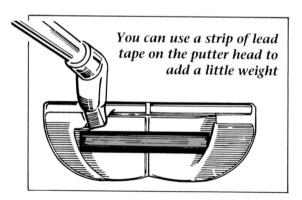

You can use a strip of lead tape on the putter head to add a little weight

The fact is that 95 per cent of shots played from within 30 yards of the hole can be executed with an action that is based on simple mechanical movements, which do not require much in the way of natural ability, and which can be learned. Consequently, the beginner can immediately putt and chip the ball well, and the established player will be able to save vital shots on and around the greens.

Build consistency in your putting

Before discussing your putting method, let us consider one factor that is often overlooked: is your putter right for you?

A quick look at the rack of putters in your golf pro's shop will tell you that most putters are manufactured at much the same length. They are made for tall golfers for one simple reason – it is easier to cut down the length of a club than to add on a few inches.

Consequently, if, like me, you are shorter than average, you probably need an inch or two cut off the end of your putter. I am 5ft 7in and have cut my putter down to 33in. If you are 5ft 1in or 5ft 2in, I would suggest trimming it even further. The purists may say that you now need to add a little weight to the head to restore the original balance. That is a detail that you might experiment with, and certainly, unless you are putting on very fast greens, a fairly heavy putter is a good idea. Too light a putter head can make you feel as though you need to 'hit' the ball along the green rather than 'stroke' it, and, as we are about to discover, the putting action is definitely a 'stroke' rather than a 'hit'.

Alignment and posture

The correct length of putter will allow you to adopt a comfortable address position close to the ball. For the moment, let us assume a flat green (or carpet – you can learn this action indoors) so that we are not concerned with the ball curving to the left or right. On a straight putt, a line across your toes should be parallel to the line of the putt, and, therefore, should miss the hole on the left (for right handers). Check yourself on this by laying two spare clubs on the green as illustrated. If you walk back behind the ball and look along the line from ball to target, you should see that the right-hand club points to the hole, and the left-hand club misses the hole on the left.

Now return to your address position, standing with your toes equidistant from your 'toe-line' club, and address a ball that is as close to the 'target-line' club as the toe of your putter head will allow.

As we will see later, you will be using your spare clubs not only for alignment purposes, but also to check the path of your putter head as you perform the putting stroke.

Thus far we are chiefly concerned with alignment and posture, and you should be holding your putter loosely at the bottom of the grip, in your right hand only. Adopt a reasonable width of stance – about 12 inches between the insides of your feet – a little wider for the longer putts. Now tip forwards from your hips, more so than you would in addressing a drive or a 5 iron shot, because here you must have your eyes over the line of the putt. A word of warning: tipping your upper body forwards should not mean lowering your head too much. Keep reasonably tall, otherwise you will cramp your putting stroke.

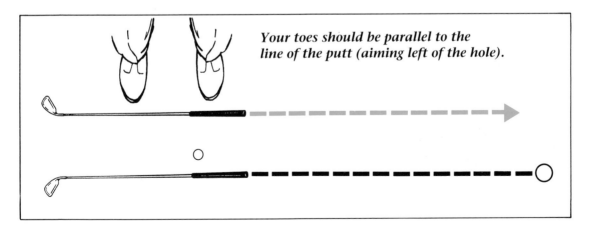

Your toes should be parallel to the line of the putt (aiming left of the hole).

Checking your position

A simple check is to hold your putter loosely in the thumb and forefinger of your right hand and bring the end of the putter grip to touch the bridge of your nose. Now lower the putter vertically, and the putter head should touch the ground on the line of the putt and just to the right of the ball. If this is so, you know that your eyes are vertically above the target line. The ball should be positioned left of centre in your stance – less than two putter head lengths from your left big toe.

The spare clubs and toe-line are parallel to the line of putt. The golfer has tipped forwards from his hips to achieve the correct putting posture and is checking that his eyes are over the line.

The grip

You are now ready to place the putter grip in both hands prior to making your stroke. If you are a beginner, you will have been working towards the correct golf grip for your driving, iron shots and pitches. If you are an established player, than let us hope that, by now, your grip for these shots is correct. In both cases you should have a grip in which the club is held primarily in the fingers of both hands, with the right palm totally covering the left thumb, and the two 'V' shapes, made by the thumb and forefinger of each hand, parallel to each other, and pointing just to the right of your chin. However, none of this is necessary, or even desirable, in your putting grip.

The end of the putter should be jammed into the palm of your left hand. The last three fingers of that hand are holding reasonably firmly, and the left-hand 'V' is pointing at, or left of, your left shoulder.

Now bring your right hand onto the club with all four fingers curled round the

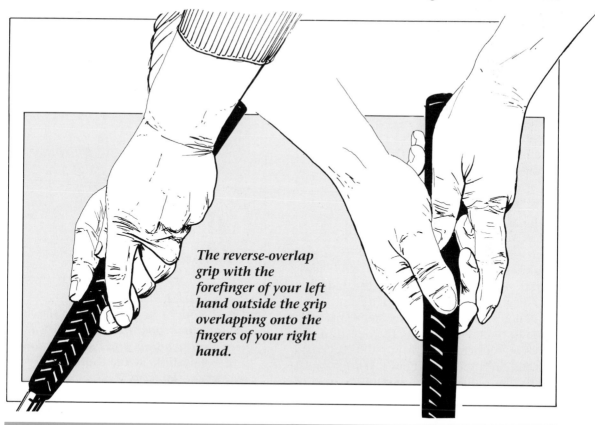

The reverse-overlap grip with the forefinger of your left hand outside the grip overlapping onto the fingers of your right hand.

grip – no overlapping or interlocking with your right little finger. It is the forefinger of your left hand that stays 'outside' your grip and overlaps onto the fingers of your right hand.

It is the position of the left forefinger that gives the putting grip its name – the reverse-overlap grip – and it is the one used by over 95 per cent of the world's top players. If you are trying it for the first time, it may feel a little strange – but persevere for a week and you will never change back!

Right hand forefinger

One final detail in the grip: your right forefinger can either curl round alongside your second finger, or separate and curl round, or, as some golfers prefer, straighten, point to the ground, and lie along the right side of your putter grip.

Addressing the ball

You are now ready to make the putting stroke. As you tip forwards to place your putter head squarely behind the ball you will need to lift your hands up and away from you slightly. This will enable you to be close to the ball, eyes over the line, and still give you room to move your hands back and through in front of your body. If your hands are too low, you will quite simply be in your own way.

Ready to putt:
The shoulder-line is parallel to the toe-line, and space has been created between the hands and body to allow a free pendulum swing. Note the reverse-overlap grip.

Your one-piece putting action

Your putter head, shaft and grip, your hands, arms and shoulders form a one-piece unit which is joined to your body at the neck. In the putting action, your head, upper body and legs are absolutely still. Your one-piece unit is moved back and forth by shoulder action, not by any conscious movement of the hands.

Your hands are merely a point halfway down the pendulum from your shoulders and neck to your putter head. Your hands, therefore, will move backwards and forwards with the stroke, but are not responsible for the movement. It is the shoulders that are the engine room of your putting action.

Move the putter backwards and forwards in front of you, making sure that there is no flapping or hingeing of the wrists. Make a dozen continuous practice movements, with no pauses, imagining a putt of about 10 yards, and look out for various points as you do this.

The putter head should be moving back a few inches past your right foot, and going through the imaginary ball to a point some way past your left foot. Your follow through should be a little longer than your backswing, and each end of your swing should be clearly defined, rather than being haphazard or sloppy.

Now watch your hands. They should be moving back and through with the putter, with no hingeing of your wrists. Feel that the back of your left hand is moving positively through towards the target.

Lastly, pay attention to your shoulders. They will be pivoting at the neck – quite generously – in order to produce the putting stroke. Meanwhile, your body and legs should be perfectly still. There should, for instance, be no movement of your hips and knees. To experience this effect, try a few practice swings, or putts, with your knees locked back as tight as you can. This will immobilize your lower body, and you will be using only your shoulders to move your arms and putter.

For your first few practice swings and putts, keep a firm grip on your putter. This will help to promote your one-piece action. Once you have perfected this, your grip can relax a little. Use about a dozen practice balls, putting them from within your parallel alignment clubs, and just putt them across an open area of green, not to a hole. At this stage, you are trying to perfect that one-piece mechanical action, and the presence of a hole will only distract you from that goal.

As you putt more and more balls, try to achieve the feeling of stroking the ball smoothly, and ever so slightly on the upstroke. This action, common to most of the best players, makes the ball roll really smoothly. As your putter head moves away from the ball, it should be nicely inside the line of the putt, moving towards, rather than away from, your right toe cap. The putter head then approaches the ball along this same inside path. Having stroked the ball away, the putter head should follow

To perfect the stroke, do plenty of continuous practice swings. Note the generous pivoting of the shoulders. The hands, meanwhile, are moving back and forth with no breaking of the wrists. Cultivate the habit of posing your end of swing position and then checking to see that it is correct. Have you kept your head, body, hips and legs still?

through to a posed end of swing position.

The path of the putter head in the follow through is a subject of debate amongst golf's theorists. Some say that it should return to an 'inside' line, i.e. left of the line of putt. My personal feeling is that it should move through along the line, or even fractionally 'outside', i.e. to the right of it. Certainly, this slight 'in-to-out' feeling is sought after by many of the game's leading putters.

The all-important follow through

As you putt more and more balls, pay particular attention to the way in which you follow through and finish the stroke. Many bad golf shots are played because the golfer sees the striking of the ball as being the object of the swing, whereas the whole concept of good golf shots is to play through

An 'out-to-in' putt (1) with the putter head returning to an inside line. An along the line putt (2) with the swing path straight down the target line. A slight 'in-to-out' swing path (3) with the putter head ending up fractionally to the right of the target line.

the ball and on into a correct finish.

As you stroke through each putt, your left shoulder pivots upwards towards your left ear, your hands swing just past your left hip, and your putter head, with no hingeing of the wrists remember, swings through perhaps 12 to 15 inches past your left foot.

You should hold this position, with eyes glued to the spot where the ball was, for a brief moment. Then, with body and shoulders held still, pivot your head to watch the ball roll. This should be a 'sideways glance' rather than a 'full face' look.

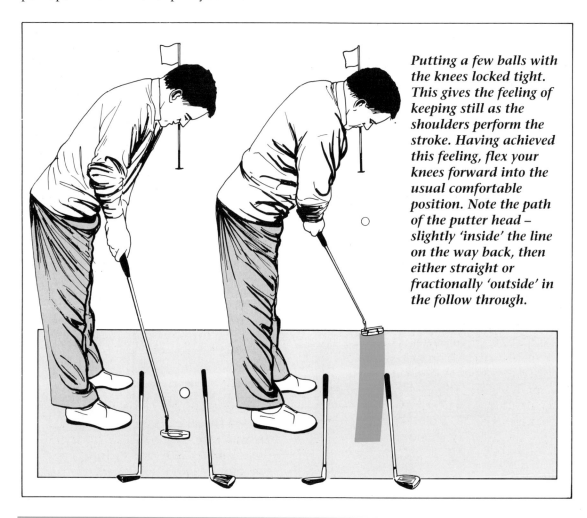

Putting a few balls with the knees locked tight. This gives the feeling of keeping still as the shoulders perform the stroke. Having achieved this feeling, flex your knees forward into the usual comfortable position. Note the path of the putter head – slightly 'inside' the line on the way back, then either straight or fractionally 'outside' in the follow through.

Putting faults

Many putts, short or long, are misdirected because the follow through is incorrect. As the golfer strikes the putt, there is a breakdown of technique. The most common faults are:

1 The left wrist collapses as the ball is 'knocked' rather than stroked.

2 The left shoulder turns to the left as the head and eyes turn towards the hole for an 'early look'.

Both of these errors cause the putter face to close, and the ball to be pulled to the left.

The universal reason for missed short putts

We shall call this Notley's Law, which reads as follows: all short putts are missed on the left – except the ones we miss on the right!

Like all daft sayings, this one has an element of truth. Short putts are missed on the left due to a technical breakdown of the putting action as the ball is struck. Missing a putt on the right is more often due to nervousness about missing it on the left. The mind is not settled. The actions are a touch nervous and twitchy. The ball is given a tentative nudge and sets off a little to the right of the intended line.

Above: An all too common result; trying to guide the ball into the hole from a short distance will cause too much upper body and head movement and a missed putt.

Note: With a sound technique and a calm mind, all your short putts will dive into the middle of the hole.

Eliminating the 'early look'

Here is a simple exercise to improve your holing out from a short distance. Set up your parallel alignment clubs to point to a hole on a level piece of green for a putt of two-and-a-half to three feet. Take up your address position and set the putter head squarely behind the ball. Have a couple of looks at the hole as your prepare to putt. Now point your nose slightly to the right of the ball, and close your left eye. The hole should have disappeared from view.

Make your smoothest putting stroke using (as you have learned) only your shoulders, arms and putter, and listen – don't look – for the ball to drop. If you stroke through the ball smoothly to the correct finishing position, you will hole this putt time and time again.

Judging the longer putts

You have now learned the mechanics of the putting stroke, and you know how to hole your short putts. As you putt more practice balls, your judgement of length should be improving too. Remember that you don't putt golf balls by giving the balls a speculative knock with the putter head, or with a jerky movement of the hands. Your shoulders are the motivating force of your putting stroke, and it is the speed, rhythm and tempo of your shoulder action that help to judge the strength of the putt.

Your putting routine

The final detail is to establish a routine for putting which starts as you walk on to the green. You should already be assessing the length of the putt and the general slope and speed of the green. Bend, or crouch, three or four paces behind the ball, looking along the line to the hole. You are looking to see whether the putt is straight , or whether the ball will break to the right or left – or both! No need to spend long on this – your first impressions are likely to be correct. Now step up alongside the ball taking up your alignment and posture, ready for your practice swings. Make three continuous practice swings looking at the hole, rather than at an imaginary ball. This is the way to gauge the rhythm and tempo for this particular putt. Now place your putter head behind the ball, move your feet forwards to the correct address position, look twice at the hole, then back to the ball and, without further delay, putt the ball with the same smooth rhythm that you have established in those continuous practice swings.

Perfect this routine on the practice green so that it becomes automatic on the course.

Chipping made easy

First of all, let's define the shot. It is that little one from just off the green where 'all you have to do' is shunt the ball on to the putting surface, and let it run up to the flag. If the terrain is flat, and you are only a few yards from the edge of the green, you play, perhaps, a 6 or 7 iron. If you are up a slope, down a bank, or behind a small bunker, you will choose a more lofted club – a 9 iron, wedge or sand wedge.

Your club selection will also depend on how far the flag is from your side of the green. If the flag is well away from you, your 6 or 7 iron will land the ball on the edge of the green, and run it to the hole from there. If the flag is close to you, you may still wish to chip the ball onto the same spot, but obviously you will not wish it to run as far. A 9 iron or a wedge will be your correct choice.

Whatever the situation, the method of playing the shot is much the same, and, fortunately for us, has much in common with the putting stroke. In fact, before going into any technical explanation of how to chip, here is your first practice exercise.

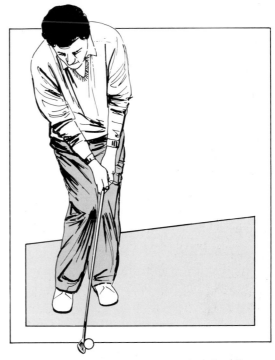

The chip is a low trajectory shot landing on the edge of the green and running to the hole from there. Using a 6 or 7 iron – chip and long roll. Using a 9 iron or wedge – chip and shorter roll. The method for playing these shots, you will be pleased to know, is the same for both.

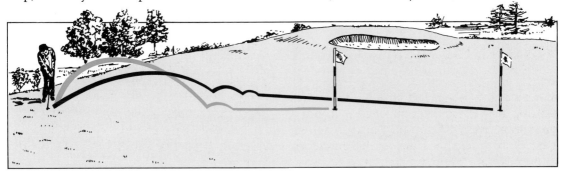

Practice exercise

You can do this indoors on a carpet or mat, and you will need your putter, an 8 or 9 iron, and four golf balls.

Drop a cushion on the floor and, from a distance of about four paces, using your Sunday-best one-piece action, putt the first two balls quite positively into the cushion, imagining a putt of fully 10 yards or more. For the second two balls, change to your iron and, still using your reverse-overlap grip, your putting address position and positive stroke, play the same two shots again. As each ball hits the cushion, you should be aware that it was airborne for the first two or three feet of its journey.

Exercise checkpoint

Your main checkpoint for this exercise is that your 9 iron head, like your putter head, should be moving back about 18 inches from the ball and through to the same distance past the ball in the follow through. Your action, as before, is mainly controlled by the tempo of your shoulders, and your end-of-swing position is held for a moment as you watch the shot. The head of your club should be low to the ground in the follow through. If you bring the club up too steeply in a conscious attempt to lift the ball, you will only top it along the ground.

This is the essence of chipping. A putt played with a putter rolls the ball along the ground, but a 'putt' played with an iron club lofts the ball for the first part of the shot. The ball is not lifted by the player. There is no scooping action with the club or hands and wrists in order to help the ball into the air. It is solely the loft of the club face passing through the ball which is responsible for the ball rising slightly for those first few feet.

So chipping is like putting . . .

As you continue to chip more practice balls, adopt a similar routine as for putting, i.e. three brisk and positive practice swings with your 9 iron (pretending that it is your putter), then step forward and play the shot with the same tempo. If anything, the action should feel a little wooden and robotic – certainly, it should not feel at all loose or sloppy.

It would be nice to say that that's all there is to it. If all our chip shots were played from perfect lies on the apron of the green, then the above method would serve us well. Unfortunately, the golf ball is inclined to sit very tight to the ground, often in a slight depression or even in an old divot mark.

It is therefore necessary, as with all iron shots, to play the chip with a slight downward strike of the club head through the ball and into the turf. On a full-length iron shot from a damp fairway, this downward strike will produce a sizeable divot. On a chip shot

If you attempt to take the ball cleanly off the grass as in (1) you will be very likely to catch the turf early and fluff the shot, or reach the bottom of your swing before the ball and top it on the way up. The illustration (2) shows the correct, slightly downward, striking of a chip shot. At the point of contact, the club shaft is angled forward towards the target. The iron head continues its downward movement (3), scuffing the turf, as the ball takes off towards the green. The club head leaves the grass (4) and continues low into the follow through.

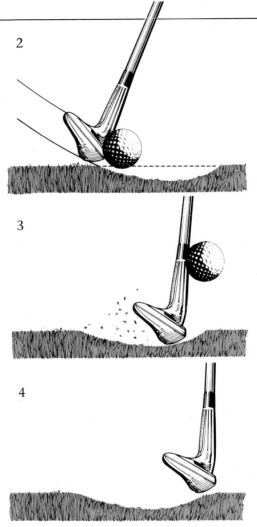

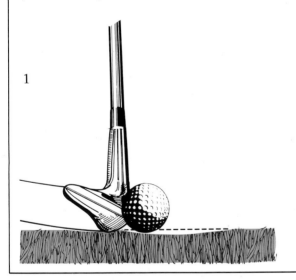

from the edge of the green, you will not be taking a divot as such, but nevertheless you should be producing a scuff mark on the turf as your club head goes down through the ball and on into the follow through. It is this slight downward strike that guarantees that the ball is raised onto the green, and it is such a vital ingredient in chipping that we must make a few adaptations to our address position to ensure that it happens.

Your chipping address position

Firstly, to make the club more manageable, and to promote control over the ball, move your hands down the club so that, still using your reverse-overlap grip, your right forefinger is curled round the bottom of the grip.

Now address the ball and angle the club shaft towards the target so that the 'spare' end of the club, above your hands, is pointing past your left hip. This puts the end of the grip nicely out of the way, and enables you to stand close to the ball. Your feet should be very close together – only a couple of inches between your heels – with your left foot turned outwards. With flexed

Indoor practice

You can practise indoors by chipping sand wedge shots from the carpet into an armchair. Make sure that the television set and the drinks cabinet are on the other side of the room! Note that if you are at all anxious and quit on the ball, you spoil the shot, but if you are confident and positive with the action, the ball chips up nicely into the chair every time.

Remember that you are not trying to lift the ball into the chair yourself. The slight downward strike and the loft of the club will do it for you.

Playing a 7 iron chip: the ball is addressed opposite the middle of the feet, and you lean towards the green (1). The backswing (2) is fairly short – it would be a little longer for a more lofted club – and is performed by the downward turn of the left shoulder. There is no movement of the knees to the right – they remain flexed towards the target. At impact (3) the knees have made a small but positive movement to the left, bringing the outside edge of the right shoe very slightly off the ground. The right knee continues to move to the target (4) as the club head drives through the ball and the turf, and on into the follow through. The finishing position should be held for a brief moment before your head turns to see the ball running to the hole.

knees, lean towards the target so that most of your weight, 80 per cent or so, is on your left foot. Your head should be over your left foot, rather than opposite the ball.

This change in address position will mean that, given the same chipping action as before, the club head will be contacting the ball just before, rather than at, the bottom of the swing.

This address position and chipping

1   2   3   4

action will take care of 95 per cent of the little shots you have to play around the green. Even a tricky one from behind a ridge or bunker is no problem. Select your sand wedge. Move your hands down the grip to about halfway (keep the reverse-overlap) and play the shot with the same wooden style that you have learned. The club head should move back to almost knee high by the downward turning of your left shoulder

– no wrist break. Then both knees, your right knee in particular, move very positively towards the target, as the brisk tempo of your shoulder action produces a positive downward strike through the ball.

Your hands and wrists should remain firm through the strike, and on into your held finishing position. The club head should remain fairly low in the follow through, well below your left knee level.

Eliminating unwanted hand action

When I watch golfers playing their chip shots, the most common fault I see is that they employ too much hand and wrist action. The wrists break in the backswing and flap into the follow through, producing a variety of indifferent results. The hands and wrists should remain firm, without being tight. What follows is an ideal exercise to promote the correct feeling.

Practice exercise

Choose your 9 iron to play a few practice chip shots, but as you set up next to the ball,

ready for a few practice swings, place a spare iron alongside the grip of your 9 iron, and take hold of both in a close approximation of your reverse-overlap grip. The head of your spare club is level with the bottom of your 9 iron grip, and the shaft goes under your left arm, past your left side.

Now try a few continuous practice swings. As your 9 iron head moves back and

This is a marvellous exercise for learning the chipping action, with or without the ball. The golfer here is chipping with a 9 iron, and using the wedge to extend the club shaft past his left side.

forth you will find that, in the follow through, the presence of the spare club eliminates any flapping of the hands.

If you hold your follow through position, you will notice that the grip of your 9 iron points past your left side. With your spare club in place, it cannot point anywhere else!

Now throw your spare club away and take another practice swing with your 9 iron, stopping at the end of the follow through. Have a look at the grip of your club. It should, as before, be pointing past your left side. If it points at your tummy button – you are still flapping!

Fit the two clubs together again and check your end of backswing position. Your 9 iron head should be just below right knee level. If you hold this position and turn your head slightly to the left, you should not be able to see the grip end of your spare club –

your upper left arm is in the way. If you can see the grip of your spare club, particularly if it is down at waist level, you have wrongly employed wrist break, instead of left shoulder turn, to take the club back.

You can now try everything you have done in your practice swings with a few balls. Using the two clubs together may seem a bit awkward at first, but you will be performing the correct chipping action.

This is one of the many exercises we enjoy at my Resident Summer Schools at Windermere Golf Club, and one fellow was so taken by it that he made himself a five-foot-long 9 iron, with a grip halfway down the shaft, for practice purposes. It is no surprise to me that he has since reported a considerable improvement in his chipping around the greens. Practising this exercise, alternating between two clubs and one, will do the same for you.

Chapter Seven

Curing
common faults

by Alasdair Barr

Golf is a difficult game to play well, and at times even the greatest players have problems with their swings. The faults have to be detected quickly and then eliminated so that the player is put back on track as soon as possible. The longer the fault lasts the more difficult it is to cure and, of course, the player's confidence is eroded. Being able to recognise the signs from the flight of the ball will help you diagnose the reason for a bad stroke.

It has to be said that most bad shots in golf stem from a faulty set up. You only have to look at Lee Trevino, of whom it could be said that he plays with a deliberate slice emanating from his set-up position. His feet, hips and shoulders are aimed deliberately to the left while his club face is aimed at the target. This deliberate 'argument' creates the left-to-right spin that he desires.

Hopefully most beginners, having followed all the correct procedures to produce an orthodox swing, will experience no problems. Sadly, this does not often happen, so when a mishit or bad shot occurs and the ball misses the desired target the fault must be found and corrected.

The simplest means of detecting the fault is for you to have a check-list that you can go through and find it by a process of elimination. However, if you search 'in the dark' hoping to find the problem two things can happen:

1 If you do not find the fault at the first attempt you will try something else and so on. In the end your brain is like scrambled eggs and all concept of the swing lost.

2 Secondly, you might just interfere with something that was correct and do the swing further damage.

It is important to understand therefore the various ball flights that can occur and appreciate that they fall into certain categories. The first factor you have to take into account is the swing path of the golf club. This is the direction the club head takes just before, during and just after impact; and it controls the direction of the ball as it starts on its journey. Then you have to appreciate how the club face relates to that swing path.

Out-to-in swing path

The correct swing path is where the club face travels from inside the ball-to-target line to square to it to inside again – this produces the perfect golf shot. From this we have a group of shots that start their journey to the left:

1 The ball that starts left and continues along that line – **a pull.**

2 The ball that starts left and then travels to the right of the target – **a slice.**

3 The ball that starts to the left and finishes on the target line – **a fade.**

These three shots are caused by a *swing path* that is called *out-to-in*. The club face will now control where the ball finishes.

1 The pull: the club face is square or in line to the swing path. As the swing path

Opposite: This demonstrates the correct inside-to-square-to-inside swing path with the blade square to the swing path and target line at the point of impact.

and club face are in agreement there is no spin on the ball so it flies straight to the left.

2 The slice: the club face is *open* (pointing to the right) to the swing path and as the two do not agree, so the spin imparted takes the ball away from the target.

3 The fade: on this particular shot the club face is square to the target line so the ball finishes on the line of the target. However, it will have spin as again the club face and swing path do not agree with each other. As I have already mentioned these shots are all from the *out-to-in swing path*.

Right: The moment of impact of the out-to-in swing path. The club on the ground represents the target line.

Out-to-in swing path

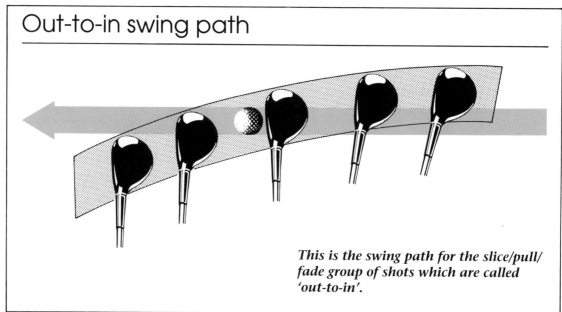

This is the swing path for the slice/pull/fade group of shots which are called 'out-to-in'.

In-to-out swing path

Now we have to take into account the shots that start to the right.

1 The ball that starts to the right and continues along that line – **a push.**

2 The ball that starts to the right and finishes to the left – **a hook.**

3 The ball that starts to the right and finishes on target – **a draw.**

All these shots are caused by a swing path that is called *in-to-out.*

1 The push: the club face is square to the swing path.

2 The hook: the club face is closed (aimed left) to that swing path.

3 The draw: the club face is square to the ball-to-target line.

Above: the moment of impact for the in-to-out swing path. The club on the ground represents the target line.

In-to-out swing path

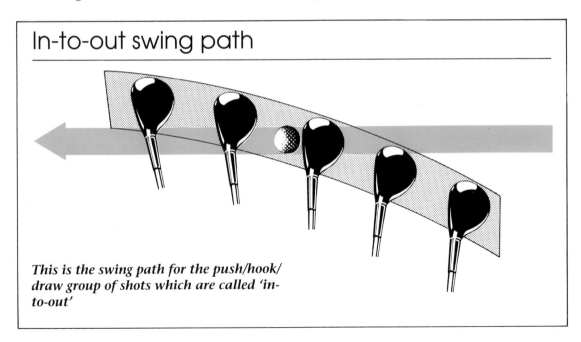

This is the swing path for the push/hook/draw group of shots which are called 'in-to-out'

For many golfers it is hard to accept that different shots can be caused by the same swing path and it is only the relationship between the club head and the swing path that changes the effect. However, hopefully that has now been explained.

Professional tip

Many highly successful tournament players have used the effects of a fade or draw to achieve their consistency. These players (like Lee Trevino) deliberately put spin on the ball to make it behave in a particular fashion so that it can travel only one way. This can be used also to keep the ball away from such hazards as out of bounds. However, a fading spin reduces the distance that most players seek so the draw or hook spin is more desirable.

So that you can see that shots fall into two particular groups and can be recognised as such:

Out-to-in: Pull
Slice
Fade
In-to-out: Push
Hook
Draw

Normally the out-to-in swing will create a descending blow and, as a result, the ball will tend to fly low. As a result of this angle of attack a skied or fluffed shot can result.

Fluffing

The club head enters the ground before the ball, and the grass between the blade and the ball dulls the power. This is more common with an iron club than a wood or metal-headed club.

Skying

The angle of descent is too steep and the ball is met by the top end of the club head. The downward blow imparts too much backspin and this forces the ball up. This is most likely to happen when playing with a wooden-headed club.

Topping

This has no set pattern but is caused when not enough of the club head reaches the ball and, as a result, the ball is driven downwards rather than upwards. This shot is prevalent amongst beginners as they mistakenly believe that the club head has to help lift the ball into the air rather than trusting this club's lift. The ball is then hit halfway up, just like taking the top off an egg.

Shanking

This is a totally devastating shot as it flies off at an alarming angle to the right. It is where the ball comes off the hosel or neck end of the club, and is usually caused by an excessive in-to-out swing thereby presenting the

hosel to the ball. A flat backswing is usually the cause of this and only by going for a more upright swing will the problem be overcome.

Shanking is caused by an exaggerated inside-to-outside swing path. Note how the hosel – where the shaft and club head meet – is being presented to the ball first.

The fix

As I mentioned earlier, most of the golfing faults are caused by an incorrect set up. We are now going to study that sequence so that we can find the faults by a process of elimination. However, if any real difficulty is experienced then the help of a PGA professional should be sought. His expertise is there for all golfers and his experience will help get you back on track as quickly as possible.

The sequence is as follows:

1 The club face
2 The grip or hold on the club
3 The stance
4 The alignment
5 The ball position
6 The swing

The correct swing path

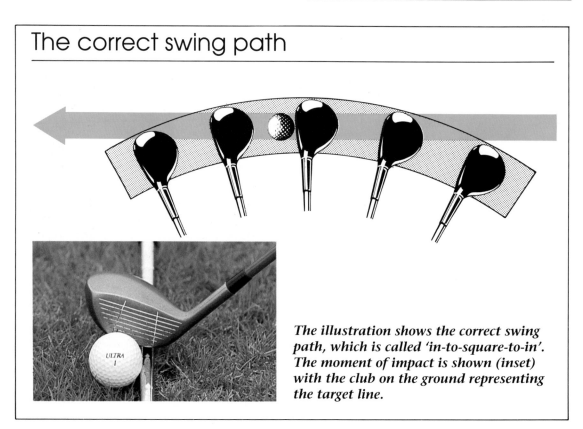

The illustration shows the correct swing path, which is called 'in-to-square-to-in'. The moment of impact is shown (inset) with the club on the ground representing the target line.

The grip

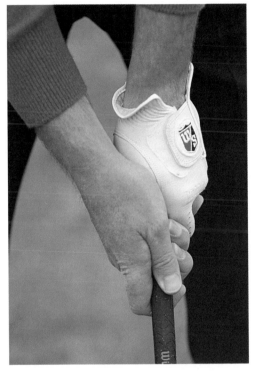

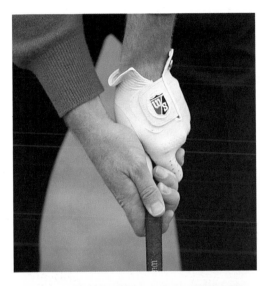

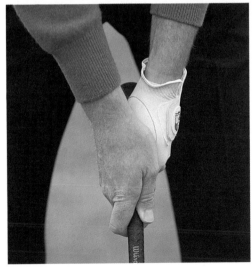

The way in which you grip the club will ultimately affect the quality of the shot you make. These photographs show a good grip (above), a strong grip (above right) and a weak grip (right). Refer to the following pages to discover the adjustments you may need to make to your grip to avoid the swing faults described.

Stance

Left: The open set up with the feet, hips and shoulders all pointing to the left. This is likely to cause the out-to-in swing path as the hands and arms can only swing along the line of the shoulders.

Right: Here the feet are aiming to the right of the target line instead of being parallel to the target line.

Ball position

Above: The correct ball position for fairway woods. The ball is positioned just inside the left heel so that it can be contacted very slightly on the upswing. Above right: The ball is too far forward in the stance with the hands positioned well behind the ball. This will cause the shoulders to open and aim to the left. Right: The reverse situation where the ball is too far back in the stance towards the right foot. The hands are too far in front of the ball causing a descending angle of attack and a 'chopping' action. The shoulders will then aim to the right (closed) of target.

Alignment

Left: The correct aim or alignment with all parts of the body agreeing with each other and with the club face. This is called the 'square' set up.

Opposite: This demonstrates how the shoulders should be parallel to the 'ball-to-target' line.

The pull/slice group (out-to-in)

The pull

1 Aim: the club face could be pointing to the left of the ball-to-target line – this is called *closed*.

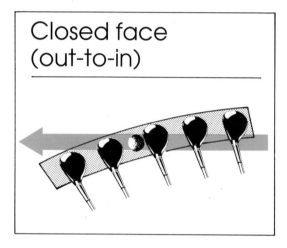

Closed face (out-to-in)

2 Grip: either or both hands are too far to the right of the grip, with more than two knuckles visible on the left hand and the 'V' on the right hand pointing to the player's right shoulder.

3 Stance: if the feet are too close together the shoulders will take over in the downswing.

4 Alignment: the feet and shoulders aim to the right. This will cause them to spin to the right to try and get the club back on line.

5 Ball position: if the ball is too close to the left foot, this will cause the shoulders to aim left.

6 Swing:
Backswing – this is started with the wrists causing the club face to open.
Downswing – the swing path is out-to-in.
Follow through – due to the above, the hands will not release to a high follow through.

The slice

1 Club face: this may point to the right called *open*.
2 Grip: either or both hands are too far to the left of the handle.
3 Stance: this is not likely to be a problem.
4 Alignment: the shoulders will point well to the left. This too is called *open*.
5 Ball position – if this is too far forward, it will also cause the above.
6 Swing:
Backswing – the club being picked up and thus the club face is open.
Downswing – the swing path will be out-to-in and this pulls the club head across the ball.
Follow through – it will be restricted and the hands and arms will be close to the body.

Opposite: This picture demonstrates that with the ball forward the shoulder line will be 'open'.

The push/hook group (in-to-out)

The push

1 Club face: could be aiming to the right.
2 Grip: the hands will not usually be a fault, but possibly a little too far to the left.
3 Stance: the feet may be a little wide causing you to restrict the follow through.
4 Alignment: the feet and shoulders are aimed to the right.
5 Ball position: the ball is too far to the right causing the hands and arms to swing along the line of the shoulders.
6 Swing: the backswing goes inside the line too quickly and you cannot get back the swing line properly on the downswing.

The hook

1 Club face: the club face could be aiming to the left or closed.
2 Grip: either or both hands are too far to the right.
3 Stance: this may be too wide causing a restricted follow through with the legs. The hands will have to take over on the through swing and this will close the club face.
4 Alignment: most likely to have the feet, hips and shoulders aimed to the right – *closed*.
5 Ball position: too far back in the stance (too close to the right foot) causing the shoulders to close.
6 Swing: the backswing will be round the body causing a very in-to-out downswing, but the hands will try to rescue the situation

by turning the club face over to get it back on line. The follow through will have the hands in a low position near the left shoulder and the balance will be very suspect, causing loss of control.

Above and opposite: These pictures show that with the ball too far back the shoulders will be 'closed'.

Skying and fluffing

As we discussed earlier, the angle of attack on to the ball is too steep and the club will be following an out-to-in swing path. The only difference between these two shots is that on the fluffed shot the club head strikes the ground before the ball, and on the skied shot the ball is struck first.

The correct action and swing path are shown above with the club head descending to strike the ball in a low sweeping angle of attack. The result of an out-to-in swing path is shown opposite at impact. The very steep angle of attack will cause a fluffed or skied shot.

Topping

Usually when the ball is topped you will be accused of lifting your head, but invariably it has nothing to do with this. Again, by following the sequence the fault can be detected.

1 Club face: this should be correct.
2 Grip: incorrect pressure could cause problems with the wrist action through impact.
3 Stance: if your stance is too wide the correct weight transfer will not be possible and you will have to strike the ball with extra wrist action. This will mean that the right hand will pass the left too quickly and the club head will then be travelling in an upward direction causing the topping effect.
4 Alignment: this will not necessarily be incorrect.
5 Ball position: this may be far too forward causing the ball to be hit excessively on the up-swing.
6 Swing: generally it is because the beginner will try to help the club head get the ball airborne, and this lifting effect causes the ball to be hit halfway up.

Shanking

This is always a very disturbing shot as the ball flies dramatically to the right. It is often called a *disease* because it saps the player's confidence so much. The ball is hit off the hosel (where the shaft meets the club head) and travels very low.

1 Club face: the club face usually is in its normal position.
2 Grip: the hands are too far to the left of the handle. This will cause the club face to open.
3 Stance: again, this cannot be blamed usually.
4 Alignment: the feet and shoulders can be aiming well to the left causing a very out-to-in swing.
5 Ball position: the ball can be positioned too far back or too far forward. Either will have a detrimental effect on the shoulder line.
6 Swing: the swing path has become so in-to-out that the flat swing causes the player to present the hosel to the ball first. The player then has to try and develop a more upright swing to create a more *on-line* attack. The shank is a very destructive shot.

Opposite: When the club face is taken back on a very flat plane (left) you may try to rescue the situation by trying to get the club head back on line thereby causing the shoulders to open. Because of the speed of the downswing, it will be overdone throwing the neck of the club head forward closest to the ball. The correct position at impact is also shown (right) with the club head, feet, hips and shoulders parallel to the ball-to-target line. It looks like the set up position but the momentum of the swing has carried the weight more to the left side.

In the shots that have been described, the fade and draw are not really considered faults as the ball finishes on the target line but I have included them when discussing the swing path earlier in the chapter as you may find a need for the deliberately controlled slice or hook as you become more advanced and may need these shots to get out of trouble, for example, by being able to bend a ball round a spinney of trees.

A final note

Do remember that if you have any lasting problems that you cannot cure alone and you feel in need of some help, the Professional at your nearest golf club is there to help so why not seek his advice? Otherwise, identify your fault and use the checklists in this chapter for easy reference and hopefully you will remedy the weakness in your swing.

The complete swing

The following sequence demonstrates the correct set up and swing with a driver or long iron. Of course, you may have to make adjustments to this swing to make allowances for your physical build, height, strength, flexibility and age.

The correct set up

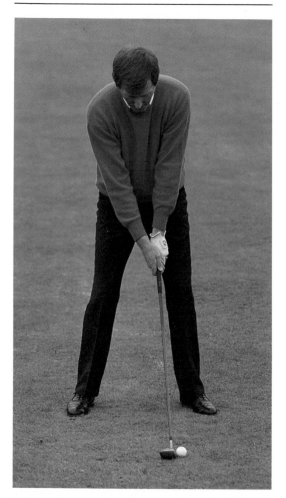

The correct position at set up (front and back views). Note the perfect alignment (aim) with the club face, feet, hips and shoulders.

The backswing

At waist level in the backswing (above) the wrists are just beginning to 'cock'. This is not a conscious movement – it happens automatically and is caused by momentum of the swing and the weight of the club head. Just let it happen! At the top of the backswing (above right) the shoulders and hips are turning the desired amount and the club shaft is parallel to the ball-to-target line. *The tension created around the hips is ready to be released. The shoulders have turned through 90 degrees (opposite) and the hips through 45 degrees, and the weight has transferred to the right side. The left arm has stayed comfortably straight and the body should feel coiled.*

The downswing and follow through

The club head is attacking the ball from the inside and the alignment achieved in the set up has been retained. The position at impact is a copy of the set up and the

follow through is relaxed. The points to look out for are as follows: the hands should finish in a high position; the weight should transfer fully to the left

shoe; the upper body should be pointing to the target or perhaps even a shade to the left indicating a full release.

Swing checkpoint

At the set up the leading edge of the club head is at right angles to the shoulders. To check that the take away has been performed correctly, this should still be the case at waist level. To check this, you make your take away and then turn your body through 90 degrees and the blade should be in the same position. It can also be checked at waist level on the follow through in the same manner. If both positions are correct, it proves that both the club and the body are working as a team and not parting company.

Take away practice exercise

To help create the correct feeling in the take away place a tee-peg in the ground six to seven inches behind the ball on the ball-to-target line. You then take the club back and try to hit the peg. This means that the club head is taken back on the line of the target and also on a line parallel to the feet, hips and shoulders. It is only when the left shoulder starts to become involved that the club head goes slightly on the inside. Keep practising this little exercise as the first two to three feet of the backswing are most important.

Chapter Eight

The mind game

by Craig DeFoy

The importance of a correct mental attitude

All golfers are aware of the difficulty of hitting good shots, especially with any kind of consistency. The physical coordination necessary to strike a golf ball the right distance and in the right direction is of a very high level, but good golf requires far more than just a high level of technical skill.

Golf is one of the few ball games that is not a 'reaction' game. The ball is stationary while you swing at it, and no time limit is placed upon the player to execute his swing. Moving ball games demand quick reactions from the player so they leave little time for thinking of how to perform the kick, catch, throw or whatever.

Furthermore, golf is not played on a playing area of fixed dimensions nor is it conducted in regular conditions. Unlike in many other sports, the weather conditions would have to be really extreme before a round of golf was called off.

All of these factors contrive to make the game of golf not only a tremendous challenge physically but surely the ultimate sporting test of the mind.

The effect of the mind in this game is absolutely crucial since we all have a unique capacity to allow both external and internal stimuli to interfere with our ability to carry out a task which we know ourselves to be capable of performing successfully. If you doubt the influence of the mind over the body, consider the following scenarios.

You are faced with a shot on the practice range with your favourite club and it poses no particular problem. However, the same shot with the same club when playing on the course in a friendly game seems only a little more difficult. Now consider how much tougher the proposition becomes when the identical shot needs to be pulled off on the final hole of a competition with the golfer in position to win.

The physical demands have remained exactly the same but the different circumstances have created mental pressures that make the shot progressively more difficult to play successfully.

The regular winners, whether at club level or at major championships, are not necessarily those who strike the ball best but those who are able to keep their concentration and also control their nerves in demanding situations. Consider therefore how much better you would play if you could improve your mental skills and not just concentrate on constantly changing your swing in a search for success!

What is the correct mental attitude?

If it is accepted that the condition of the mind is all important in golf, what is the ideal mental attitude you should seek to acquire? The most difficult aspect of the game is that you are only spending a few minutes during the course of a round actually swinging a club at the ball. A typical round takes anywhere from three to four-and-a-half hours and most of that time you are apt to let your mind wander and are susceptible to all kinds of distracting thoughts. Finding a way of maintaining concentration therefore is very important, and we shall deal with that shortly.

In most sports adrenaline plays a big part. Natural excitement and a keenness to do well will create this adrenaline which adds a little speed and power to the body. These are the last things needed in golf since an extra surge of energy is likely to make you swing more quickly and therefore probably mishit the ball more often.

Calm awareness

The ideal mental condition for the golfer is one of calm awareness. In this mode you might be aware of outside occurrences or distractions but they will not be allowed to interfere with your thinking or swinging. This perfect state of mind is not easily achieved – ask any tournament professional – but with a little practice you can go a long way towards bringing it about.

Treat every shot the same

Perhaps the first thing to realise is that every golf shot carries the same value – a two-inch putt counts just the same as a 200-yard drive. Having said this, we are all aware that some shots during the course of a round can seem to take on a special significance. When faced with such a shot you will often tend to either rush it in a bid to get it over with, or study it for too long and try too hard to hit it correctly. Either of these approaches will inevitably lead to a poor shot, so what you must do is develop an identical approach to every shot you play.

All golf fans will be familiar with the pre-shot routines of the top players. It is easy to recognise the stars even before they swing the club because their approach to a shot never varies. Nick Faldo, for example, has a highly individual and distinctive approach to the ball which, if timed, would certainly last for a very precise number of seconds and would not vary whether he was hitting his first tee shot of the day or his approach to the final green of a major championship. These mannerisms become very much an integral part of every player's game and are vital for maintaining rhythm and in keeping the golfer's nerves under control. The familiarity of a pre-shot routine acts as a kind of crutch during times of pressure, helping to make each shot appear the same. The more you can cultivate the feeling that a shot is just a shot – no more or less important than any other – the more consistently you will play.

Whilst the physical parts of a player's pre-shot routine are very recognisable, what is less obvious is the mental side. The number of waggles a golfer takes or the angle at which he approaches the golf ball may be vital but these alone are of limited value. Every top golfer has a mental routine that he has cultivated and it is absolutely essential that you should develop one too if you are to play your best golf. Let us look into this mental process in some detail so that through understanding a little more about how the mind works, you can use this knowledge to perfect your own approach to the game.

It is generally accepted that the left side of the brain is the analytical part which takes care of our organizational and planning skills. The left side is responsible for assessing received information and using this data for the formation of any plan or coming to any decision we might take. These are very important skills in a complicated game like golf where every round is made up from a number of decisions in terms of club selection or choice of target area and so on. The danger in being too left brained is that you can easily over-analyse your swing and will thereby tend to lose the natural flow of your game.

The right side of the brain is the intuitive side and is responsible for all visual and kinesthetic skills. Touch and feel are absolutely crucial to the golfer as is the ability to use your imagination when faced with an unusual shot. This is all the domain of the right side of the brain.

Both hemispheres are constantly in use throughout our everyday lives but to improve your golf you need to use both left- and right-brained skills in the correct sequence.

When about to play any golf shot we are subjected to various pieces of information, such as yardage, lie and weather conditions. This information must be analyzed and a decision made as to the club to be used and the type of shot to be attempted. This is very much a left-brained process, but at this stage analysis ends and intuition must take over.

The next step is to convert your decision into a mental picture and this is absolutely vital. You must learn to visualize the ball leaving the centre of your club face and flying towards the target with exactly the type of flight that you desire. Once you have this mental picture of your perfect shot firmly in mind it is time to move onto the final stage – hitting the ball. The visualization process is very much the domain of the right side of the brain and this is how you ought to be hitting the ball – relying on your natural, intuitive skill rather than trying to work out how to swing. Most golf teaching is concentrated on the physical movements necessary to swing the club effectively and has a strong left-brained bias. This tends to instill in the pupil a mistrust of his natural ability and a tendency towards over-analysis of his swing. The result is often a rather

Professional tip

Don't think of *how* to swing, but think of *where* to hit the ball, and your golf is sure to improve. Make a plan, form the plan into a picture and then just give your natural talent a chance.

anxious movement lacking any real rhythm or timing. To play your best golf you must be very clear about the shot you are attempting and have a really strong awareness of your target. So once you have found your picture simply move in to the familiar physical part of your pre-shot routine and allow yourself to swing the club almost as if on auto-pilot.

Concentration

One of the most difficult aspects of golf is the length of time it takes to play a round. The average length of time taken to play 18 holes is between three and four-and-a-half hours. A common mistake is to try to concentrate throughout this period but golf is after all a social game and anyone who walks around all the time staring at the ground with a furrowed brow is likely to find it difficult to find playing partners!

Since the game is so difficult, you obviously have to concentrate on what you are doing otherwise your score is bound to suffer, but how do you strike a balance between being sociable and keeping your mind on your game? The answer is, of course, to concentrate whilst playing your shots and relax in between them since hours of grim mental struggle are hardly fun and it is totally unreasonable to expect to maintain such a level of intensity for that length of time anyway.

Concentration is best defined as a state during which your mind is focused upon one thing to the exclusion of all else. If you cast your mind back to your school days, you'll remember that the lessons in which you learned best and the subjects you most enjoyed were the ones that proved most interesting. Forcing yourself to concentrate never does seem to work so the main thing is to find each shot interesting. If you find your mind wandering when about to play a shot, stand back and try to find something about the target on which you can focus, and you will find yourself thinking back in the present and able to give that shot your best effort.

The mental and physical pre-shot routine has been discussed already and when you consider all the variables that affect each shot then you should not find it too difficult to keep your attention focused where it should be as long as you don't make unreasonable demands on yourself.

This introduces the vital point – for just how long can you sustain sufficient interest during a round? Very little of your time is spent actually hitting the golf ball – only some three to four minutes, in fact. Use the time spent walking between shots to relax your mind and body and enjoy the company of your playing partners and the beautiful surroundings in which golf courses are set and only begin to think about your next shot as you approach the ball. As you arrive at the ball, take note of all the factors that are going to have a bearing on the shot and slip into your pre-shot routine as discussed earlier. Once the ball is on its way, nothing you can do will alter its path so don't waste your mental energies on the causes or the outcome. Simply observe the shot and then switch your attention onto something else. Giving your mind a little respite in this way can only be a good thing as it will keep you fresh and ready to switch onto the next shot.

Learning to switch your concentration on and off in this way ensures that your system does not become overloaded and you maintain your interest in each shot much more easily. This is much less stressful than 'trying to concentrate' for the whole round and will prove far more effective too. So remember that golf is a game to be enjoyed; having fun is much more interesting than 'trying'. Bear this in mind and your concentration will come much more naturally, and so will lower scores!

Practice makes perfect

When a group of international amateur golfers was recently asked "How big a part does the mind play in the game of golf?" the answers ranged from 50 per cent from one player to between 80 and 90 per cent from most of the others. When asked the next question, "How much of your practice time do you devote to mental training?" the response was very interesting. Almost all the players said that they spent little or no time working on their mental approach because they did not know where to begin.

You might think that what applies to top internationals does not necessarily hold true for the average player and in some ways

this might well be true. However, if you accept that the things that have been discussed so far in this chapter can have a positive effect on your golf game, then you must also accept that they cannot all be incorporated overnight and therefore some practice is going to be necessary.

Simply being aware of using your mental abilities correctly will undoubtedly help your game but constant repetition is essential before these good habits become engrained. The great advantage is that mental training can be carried out almost anywhere that is peaceful and need not take up much of your valuable time. A few moments in your favourite arm chair planning your way round your home course and playing each hole in your mind can be a very fruitful exercise, particularly if you are about to play that course on the following day. This 'mental rehearsal' before a competition is something in which almost all good players indulge.

The art of visualization, which is so vital to good golf, can also be practised in this way. The better you are able to mentally 'see your shots', the more successfully you are likely to play them.

This is not the place to discuss all the forms of mental exercise that are available, but relaxation techniques and meditation whether through something as popular as yoga, for instance, or simply learning to relax the mind and body whenever you have the opportunity will obviously enable you to achieve the state of mental alertness that is conducive to successful golf and maintaining concentration.

Chapter Nine

Tactics and strategy

by Mark Thomas

Golf has become a very technical game in recent years with the manufacturers now producing equipment to suit all shapes and sizes. Unfortunately once the player has bought his/her tailor-made set of golf clubs and has the 'go-further' golf balls teed up ready to go, there is little thought as to how exactly he/she is going to play the course. After spending a considerable amount of money on new equipment, many golfers expect instant success and lower scores. Sadly, this is normally not the case, and they soon become very disappointed. They might go back to their golf professional and complain or, better still, have some supplementary lessons, but even these will not guarantee lower scores.

The only way to improve your scores is to improve your thinking about the round ahead, and by this I mean having a game plan: working on your strategy as well as your swing. This is an area of golf that is rarely considered by most golfers, be they scratch or high-handicap players. Over the next few pages, you can discover some ways of improving your golf so that not only will your scores be lower, but also your enjoyment of the game will be increased. We will explore how you can save shots, from simple social golf up to competitive medal rounds, and also how to approach individual holes in different ways.

There are many different types of competition in golf, but strokeplay (Medal) and matchplay (Holes) are the most popular. There are ways in which you can improve your tactics and strategy when faced with certain situations during these two competitions. Obviously, it is difficult to cover every situation, but we are going to tackle the most common ones that you will encounter.

Strokeplay

'The object of strokeplay is to get round the golf course in the least amount of shots possible.' This might seem an obvious statement, but it is often too easily forgotten by club golfers and, sometimes, even by professional golfers.

Unfortunately, most club golfers, unlike professionals, have very few opportunities to play medal (strokeplay) rounds of golf, as usually they are playing social golf with their friends and not having to keep a score. So when the monthly medal comes around, they are not accustomed to planning their round and scoring, and this can lead to mistakes they would not normally make, whereas new players who are trying to get their first handicap to join a club have to add up every shot they play and know from the start that every stroke will count.

I have often heard the classic statement: "If only I could play the 16th better, I would have a good score, but I just cannot play that hole." However, do these golfers think about playing the hole differently next time? Probably not. This is where a game plan is needed. It is no good trying to play the course the same way every time if it does not work.

The first thing that club golfers should remember is that their handicap is there to help them on the course, and is not just a

Get off to a comfortable start; if you try too hard, your first shot may go off line and end up in the rough to either side of the fairway. Try to hit the ball down the middle and aim for accuracy – not distance. You will ultimately save shots.

number to try and beat by three, four or five shots. If the handicap is used correctly and a game plan is devised, more often than not you will find that all the handicap is not needed, and so the final score will be a few shots less than the handicap.

> **Note:** Most of the shots lost on the course usually come either at the beginning or the end of a round, and this is probably due to having a big score (7 or 8 etc) on one or two holes at the wrong time.

Let us deal first with the start of the round. Probably for most players the first shot off the tee is the first shot for over a week. So it is hardly surprising when that first shot goes off line and into trouble; a few more swipes up to the green, chip on, three putts and you have an 8! So now you are faced with the rest of the round and trying to not only save shots on other holes but also enjoy yourself.

Here is what I suggest you try next time there is a medal round at your course. Firstly, select a club that you feel confident with and that should keep you in play. If your partners ask you why you are not taking the driver, tell them this is all part of your new 'game plan' to get off to a better start. Having put the ball in play, you now need to select a club that is going to put the ball up towards the green. You do not have to hit it onto the green if the distance is still too far to risk a long club. Remember that all

you are trying to do is to get off to a more comfortable start, and if that means playing for a drop shot then so be it. At least it is only one shot, not three or four like last time, and with your handicap there are plenty of holes left to make a few pars.

You may need to use this tactic for a few more holes until you feel warmed up and settled into your round. Remember that it is 'how many' *not* 'how it looks'. I am sure you will find that lower scores are easier to come by if you adopt this approach.

If, however, you find that all your shots are being lost at the *end* of the round, try and think about how they are being dropped. Is it a case of:

1 Thinking that all the hard work has been done and all you have to do is finish?
2 Hitting the 'wrong' shot and then not playing the 'right' shot to get you back in play?

Most of the time, I am sure that it is the second reason – not playing the right shot after a wrong shot – and this can happen at any time on the course, not just at the end of a round. I shall give a couple of examples that I expect you will recognise.

1 Playing a par 3, you have put your ball into a bunker not far from the pin, but it requires a delicate shot to get close and you leave the ball in the sand after a couple of attempts to get it out. Eventually you finish with a 5 or 6, and that is the end of the good score.
2 Having hit a wayward tee shot the ball finishes in the rough. You now take a club that you not only hope will get the ball out of the rough but will also put it on the

green. This, of course, does not happen, and you proceed to put the ball deeper and deeper into trouble, eventually finishing the hole with a total score that has ruined any chances you had of doing well.

With the benefit of hindsight, everybody realises the mistakes they have made, but do you ever think about the potential problems before they happen? Usually it is only the very clever players who are aware of what might happen, and they are the ones who will perform well more often.

The following suggestions are for you to try next time you are faced with the problems outlined above:

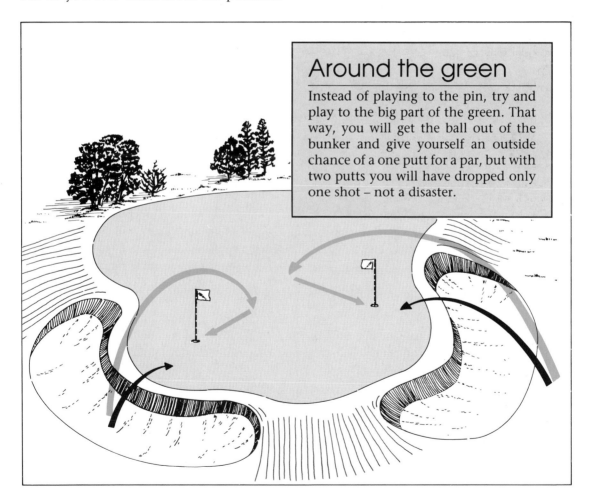

Around the green

Instead of playing to the pin, try and play to the big part of the green. That way, you will get the ball out of the bunker and give yourself an outside chance of a one putt for a par, but with two putts you will have dropped only one shot – not a disaster.

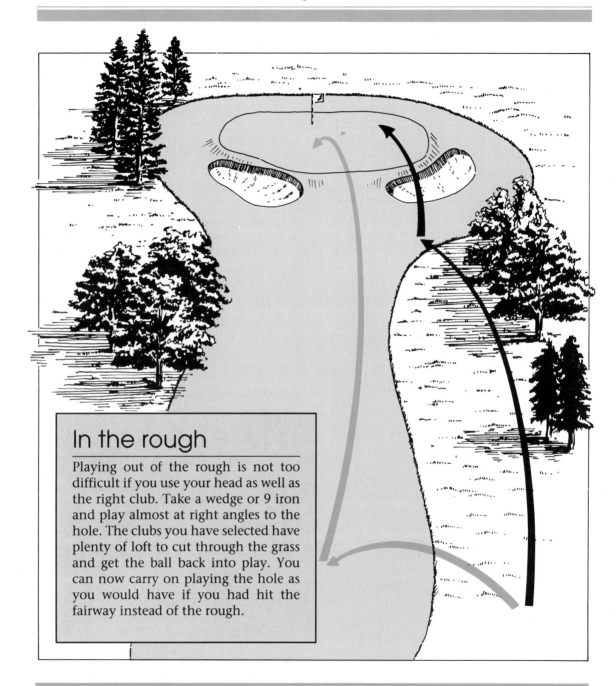

In the rough

Playing out of the rough is not too difficult if you use your head as well as the right club. Take a wedge or 9 iron and play almost at right angles to the hole. The clubs you have selected have plenty of loft to cut through the grass and get the ball back into play. You can now carry on playing the hole as you would have if you had hit the fairway instead of the rough.

Professional tip

The secret to better scores, if there is one, is keeping the ball in play, and putting it onto the fairway and away from trouble. This can be achieved only by using the right tactics, working out your game plan, and trying to play within your given ability. If you try to play shots that are outside your limitations, your scores will not get lower, so make a decision to play more percentage golf – not risky golf.

Using this type of strategy when faced with possible disaster will not only save you strokes but will also help increase your confidence, as you are now using your brains as well as your body.

All top professionals would adopt this type of strategy when faced with potential disaster. They are aware of what could happen if the risk they take does not come off. They are also not afraid to drop the odd shot because they can make it up with a birdie on the holes ahead. You can learn from their example; after all, if top pros think before they play the next shot, so must you as a high-handicapper. All this advice adds up to good on-course tactics. What you don't want to do is to drop more than one shot at a time.

Those are just two common examples that happen regularly to club players. So the next time this type of problem occurs be aware of what might happen and play the more sensible shot – it will save you many shots in the long run.

Matchplay

Matchplay is played either singly or with a partner, and the object is to win as many holes as you can by achieving a lower score than your opponent(s) at each hole, i.e. you make a par 4 at the first hole and your opponent makes a 5, so you have won that hole and are now 'one up'. You keep playing like this until you have gained more holes than you have lost, and you have won more holes than are left to play, i.e. if you have won five holes but only four are left to play, then you have won the game five up with four to play (5/4). The matchplay game can be a little more complicated than strokeplay as you and your opponent will have handicaps and therefore the giving and taking of shots comes into force. Your local professional will be able to explain this in more detail to beginners but if you have a handicap, you will be well acquainted with the rules of matchplay.

How to play better matchplay golf

Unlike strokeplay, matchplay can be played with a lot more 'bravado'. It lends itself to 'risk taking' and an 'attacking' type of golf, and because of this approach your game plan and tactics are somewhat different from those used in strokeplay.

The first thing to remember is that this is not a game of strokes, i.e. counting every shot until the end of the match – you are going to have good holes and bad holes in matchplay. So do not worry if you take a big score at a particular hole, as the result is a loss only at that hole, and you start again on the next tee.

At the start

If you and your opponent are of equal standard (i.e. there are no shots being given or taken because of a handicap difference) and it is your turn to tee off first, always think of getting the ball in play. Do not worry about distance, as just by putting the ball on the fairway, you will immediately put your opponent under pressure to do the same.

This, of course, is 'good tactics', as he may try too hard to do the same and thereby be forced into making a mistake which will give you an immediate advantage – good matchplay golf.

What you want to avoid is to start by giving away the advantage of teeing off first. To win the first hole in matchplay will always build your confidence for the rest of the round. Try and keep this strategy for the first few holes. If, however, your opponent, through his good play, manages to win the first couple of holes, you are now in a situation that will require different 'tactics'. Just by seeing how your opponent has played those opening holes will give you some indi-

In the first few holes of matchplay you should only take risks (1) if you start losing too many holes otherwise take the safe route (2) to avoid giving away any advantage to your opponent.

Matchplay

Some people sat that Matchplay is the true game of golf as you are playing golfer to golfer, head to head, and not having to worry about all the other competitors on the course. Matchplay can be far more exciting than strokeplay to watch, especially at the level of the World Matchplay Championship which always produces exciting and attacking golf from the professionals.

cation of his form, and if it seems likely that he is going to play well for the rest of the round, you are going to have to take a few more 'risks' to win the holes back. By 'risk' I mean trying to play a few shots that you would not normally play in a medal round because of the possible danger of disaster. However, in matchplay you can lose only one hole, not three or four shots as in strokeplay, and if it looks as though your opponent is going to play well you have nothing to lose.

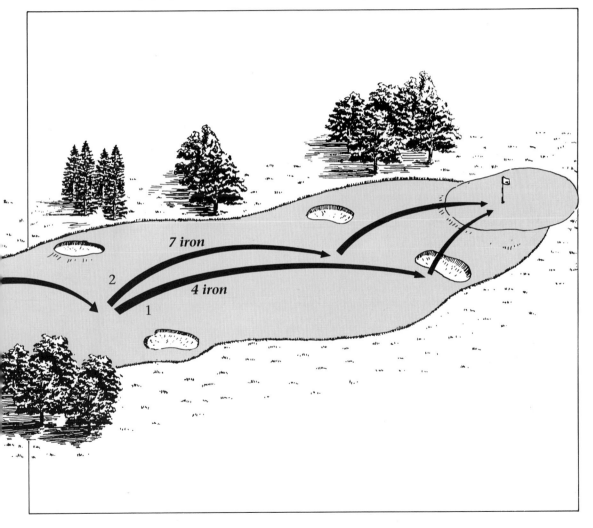

An example of a typical 'risk' shot is when you are playing a par 3 hole, and you take plenty of club, perhaps one more than you think it is (a 4 instead of a 5 iron) and really play for the pin, not just the green.

Try and put the ball down the hole; if the shot comes off and you win the hole back, think how good you will feel and how much confidence you will gain. Your opponent will notice your new-found confidence and

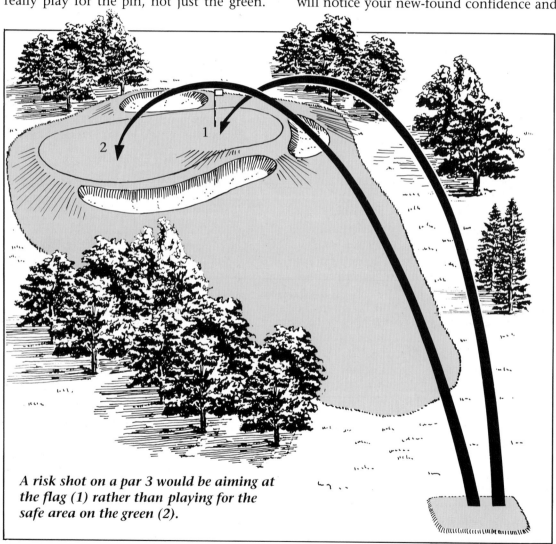

A risk shot on a par 3 would be aiming at the flag (1) rather than playing for the safe area on the green (2).

probably start to think that the match is not going to be as easy as he thought. Many a match has been won by a player taking a chance and it paying off. If, however, the 'risk' fails, don't worry but gain confidence from the fact that at least you tried.

Professional tip

The secret of playing good matchplay golf is to watch your opponent to see how he is playing and then adapt your game accordingly. Remembering that matchplay is different from stroke-play, you are really trying to put your opponent under pressure: for example, by hitting the fairway first, hitting the green first, putting up close to the hole first (only if you are first to putt – hopefully you won't be). All these tactics make for good, sound matchplay golf. But always bear in mind that you are playing another person, not the course, and at times your tactics and game plan will be completely different from those used in strokeplay.

I hope that this advice will be of help to your golf. Always remember that after all the tactics and game plans, the most important thing is that golf is a game for enjoyment and relaxation, not a matter of life or death, so when you next play and things are not going well, regardless of what you try to do, perhaps the best strategy to take would be to simply smile, accept that it is not going to be your day and think how much better it will be the next time you will play.

Tips to improve your strategy

1 Try to play the first hole with a medium iron off the tee, just to get off the tee and into play.
2 Only take a few clubs out one day (half set). This will make you play more types of shots than usual.
3 Play to the centre of the green, not the pin.
4 Do not take chances with pitching and chipping – be bold, get the ball on the green.
5 Put your driver away and use only a 3 or 5 wood off the tee.
6 Take one more club than you think, and try to hit the ball through the green.
7 Play to drop a shot on long holes; forget pars (high-handicap players).
8 Playing two balls one after the other: play one against the other. With one ball you play the 'attacking and risk-taking' shot, and with the other, the 'conservative and safe' shot. This will give you a good indication of which style of play best suits your game. Then you can adopt that approach in any forthcoming competitions.

Index

Index